The SUCCESSFUL MANAGER

The SUCCESSFUL MANAGER

HOW TO GET THE BEST OUT OF YOUR TEAM

MYLES DOWNEY
with IAN HARRISON

An imprint of
Srishti Publishers & Distributors

Srishti Publishers & Distributors
A unit of AJR Publishing LLP
212A, Peacock Lane
Shahpur Jat, New Delhi – 110 049

editorial@srishtipublishers.com

First published in the Indian Subcontinent by Bold,
an imprint of Srishti Publishers & Distributors in 2024

First published in English language as The Enabling Manager
by LID Business Media Limited, UK in 2022

10 9 8 7 6 5 4 3 2

By arrangement with LID Business Media Limited.

This edition is for Sale in the Indian Subcontinent only

Printed and bound in India

Contents

Introduction

Here's our promise to you: adopt the approach spelled out in this book and your team will hit their goals more often, get it right more often, learn more and enjoy the time they spend at work. And you'll open doors for your progression, develop yourself and enjoy a more fulfilling life.

Most people don't like being managed. It has been suggested that the three things that people dislike most at work are time spent travelling to work, time spent travelling from work and, most of all, time spent with their manager. It has also been shown in a number of studies that it is the manager who is the primary cause of most people leaving their jobs.[1]

On the flip side, according to the Chartered Management Institute, training managers can increase performance within an organization by up to 32%.[2] Then there's a Gallup report that shows the factor that most influences people's engagement with work is their manager's behaviour.[3]

One final statistic: 71% of UK organizations admit that they fail to effectively train first-time managers.[4] That's like sending a teacher into a classroom of teenagers without any teacher training – the teacher may well know their subject inside out, but that will be irrelevant if they do not have the skills required to teach.

Once you've digested all of this information, you stop wondering why most people don't like being managed.

The management culture in most large organizations is still founded in a 'command-and-control' approach. This doesn't work so well in the 21st century, because people are less compliant than their parents were and have a greater sense of their own autonomy – they are less respectful of position, authority and hierarchy. It also doesn't work because command-and-control tends to create a climate of fear and suppression, and that kills performance.

What's required is a culture and management approach that creates the conditions for high performance and innovation, where self-expression and learning are possible and where work is meaningful – a culture that's appropriate for the people in work now. We call it align and enable.

Align and enable includes three skills at which the team manager should be proficient: Lead, Manage and Coach. Lead is about the *Why*: the organization's purpose and goals, and how the individual team member relates to them. Manage is about the *What*: the objectives and standards the team member works to. Coach is about the *How*: the team members' approach to achieving their objectives.

When the *Why*, *What* and *How* are clear, most of the conditions for high performance are met. For the team member, this translates into more meaning in their work and therefore more engagement. It increases the likelihood that they'll be successful and, along the way, develop themselves and their skills. Work becomes more fulfilling. For the organization, it means more productivity, more innovation and better decisions made more quickly. Greater effectiveness and efficiency across large numbers of people is a really meaningful goal for any organization.

In this book, we have put a significant emphasis on Coach. This is because this is where our approach differs most from command and control. Coaching is key to enabling. It's where the team member does their own thinking, facilitated by the manager (or any other person). This is how ownership and responsibility for objectives, projects and tasks are taken on by the team member.

In our view, there's a whole lot of coaching going on in most organizations. Any time a manager has a conversation about How to perform a task or solve a problem, that's coaching – it's just not labelled as such and is therefore not as effective as it could be. Imagine if managers understood that they are coaching a lot of the time, understood that coaching requires a different kind of conversation and became even fairly good at it. That would transform work and people's experience of it.

We've made our promise, and here's the call to action. Read the book, act on what you learn. Make a difference every day.

CHAPTER 1

Time for Change

People's expectations of their work have been developing and changing, and old models of management are becoming less and less effective. However, the most recent generations to enter the workplace provide a clear indication of what is needed to lead our teams successfully.

Old models don't work

There is nothing quite like a global pandemic to increase the pace of change in the workplace. The Covid-19 pandemic has led to dramatic shifts in working practices and the expectations of people in work. Many of the changes were already in progress before Covid brought the world to a standstill. What the pandemic did was to dramatically disrupt fixed patterns of behaviour over a long enough timescale to allow new patterns to take root. The rest of the 2020s will reveal which of the changes become the 'new normal,' but patterns of work will never be the same again.

Even before Covid, the business climate was beset by disruption. Fast-changing technology, the ever-increasing speed of change, more and more interdependencies across industries, and rapidly evolving geopolitics had led to the world in which we operate being described as volatile, uncertain, complex and ambiguous (VUCA). To cope with this, today's business organizations need an approach that is more flexible, responsive and agile, enabling better decisions to be made more quickly. And such a different way of working requires a different approach to the way you manage your team.

Part of the problem is that there is little consensus on what such an approach should be, not least because we are stuck in a 20th-century mindset. As an example, most attempts to build a 'coaching culture,' a route some organizations have taken in response to these changes, falter when they bump into the need – real or felt – of many managers to be in control.

Changing expectations

Before the pandemic, much was written about the challenges of millennials and Gen Z entering the workforce. They have sometimes been made out to be generations in which a strange and sudden shift has taken place. They challenged traditional models of leadership and management, wanted different things from their careers and their work–life balance. But these desires did not suddenly emerge as novelties in these generations; they are the natural progression of changes that have been unfolding since the middle of the 20th century. And what the millennials and Gen Z began to ask for – development and growth, transparency and connection, work that has meaning and purpose, and empowerment – are now what everyone is looking for.

One of the things that marked out the 20th century, in the world of work, was the drive for efficiency, and it presents us with a useful insight into the limitations of the 20th-century mindset. The drive for efficiency has been called 'Fordism' after its famous early exponent: Henry Ford. His introduction of the production line transformed manufacturing and started a race for ever-increasing efficiency. Fordism evolved into Total Quality Management, then Business Process Re-engineering (BPR), then Six Sigma and Lean manufacturing. (Six Sigma is an approach to process improvement in which 99.99966% of all products are expected to be defect free.)

Efficiency has brought many benefits. However, there are costs; in 1995 Thomas H Davenport, one of the leading exponents of BPR, wrote an article that described BPR as "The Fad that Forgot People."[5] People end up being secondary, part of the process and ultimately disposable in service of efficiency. It is not surprising, then, that a major issue facing business today is a lack of productivity arising from a disengaged workforce. But that is not the only cost: efficiency tends to drive compliance, and compliance is the enemy of innovation and creativity. Efficiency has now been taken as close to perfection as can be imagined, so where can improvement and development come from today? The conventional answer is 'innovation.' But a workforce that has been trained to comply – for years – cannot easily switch on innovation.

In 1911 Frederick Taylor, the father of scientific management and a forerunner of Henry Ford, referred to carrying out repetitive tasks as "soldiering."[6] The process-based management styles that developed during the 20th century were all designed to enable managers to get the best out of their "soldiers." The job of the manager was to refine and enforce the processes to achieve the greatest possible efficiency. Taylor theorized that "soldiers" would always work to the minimum level of productivity that went unpunished. This meant that the work of a manager was to constantly raise the minimum acceptable productivity of the "soldiers."

Even as efficiency experts were developing their models, other changes were happening in society that would challenge this idea that workers are best managed as soldiers whose job it is to obey commands without question. Not least among these changes were improvements in education and general prosperity.

In the UK, for example, the post-war creation of the welfare state delivered health care and education that were free at the point of delivery and a benefits system intended to avoid the kind of poverty experienced in the 1930s. As the country rebuilt itself, more and more people enjoyed a level of prosperity that put a secure roof over their heads and guaranteed that there would be food on the table. People were freed from worrying about their physical needs and could turn their attention to higher-level needs, such as respect, autonomy and purpose. As a result, for a lot of people, employment has become about more than meeting basic needs.

As their parents became more secure, more and more young people were able to extend their education such that, in 2018/19, over 50% of 18 to 30 year-olds in the UK had participated in higher education.[7] A more educated workforce is a workforce that has higher expectations of their working life. When it comes to considering their future careers, "soldiering" is not on the radar.

These changes in attitude were emerging throughout the latter half of the 20th century, but it was the entry of millennials into the workplace that brought the issue to a head. Born between 1981 and 1996, these were the children of the post-war generation, whose parents had been raised in the increasing prosperity of the 1960s and 1970s.

In the 20th century, organizational life was marked by a culture of strict compliance and of 'doing my best,' held in place by an approach to leadership that arose from a command-and-control mindset. This model of leadership is neither appreciated nor understood by those who have entered the workforce since the year 2000, and for the general population it is no longer conducive to high levels of performance.

Changing technology

We cannot move on without acknowledging that the changes accelerated by the pandemic were intrinsically linked to developments in technology. When Eric Yuan founded Zoom Video Communication Inc in 2011, he could not have imagined that nine years later his business would be worth $35 billion or that to 'Zoom' would have become a globally recognized verb.[8] The way businesses were able to adapt so rapidly to the pandemic would have been impossible without the technologies that had emerged over previous decades.

Similarly, it is these technologies that will become even more important as hybrid and remote-working models become the new normal for many people. This means that, as a manager, you are likely to find yourself leading people with whom you have far less face-to-face time.

While some companies have reached for spyware technologies to bolster their command-and-control management culture,[9] these will rapidly become unattractive places to work. Technology will continue to increase the level of autonomy people expect while doing their work.

A message that cannot be ignored

Needless to say, much of the business world has resisted the change that is required: when you've tasted power, it's difficult to give it up! This brings us back to millennials. Initially, they were seen as difficult to attract, even more difficult to retain, impossible to manage and a threat to the prevailing business culture. The business press described them as demanding, disengaged with work, easily distracted and holding a naive sense of entitlement.[10]

But look deeper and you will find that millennials want work that has meaning and purpose, empowerment to get on with the job, development and growth, a path to promotion, and the freedom to work where and when they want[11] – desires that became much more widely embraced during the Covid-19 pandemic. These changes are likely to stick, not simply because they make life more pleasant but also because they make work itself more productive and more fulfilling. Maybe the real difference between previous generations and those who have entered the workforce since 2000 is that the latter have had the courage to say, "This way of working, well, it isn't working."

We argue that we are at an inflection point where the change in the curve can just be detected, and what comes next is slowly emerging. Rather than presenting a problem, the much-maligned millennials are pointing the way. Their desire for work that has meaning, growth and empowerment requires an approach to leadership that seeks to align and enable rather than command and control.

A THOUGHT EXPERIMENT TO TRY

Think of a time when you found your work rewarding. How were you being managed at the time?

Think of a time when you dreaded Monday morning and every week was a countdown to Friday. How were you being managed?

Finally, if you were joining a new team, how would you want to be led?

WANT TO KNOW MORE?

Generation Z: A Century in the Making by Corey Seemiller and Meghan Grace[12]
This well-researched book takes a deep dive into the making of the latest generation to enter the workforce and their defining characteristics.

The Purpose Economy by Aaron Hurst[13]
In this easily accessible book (there's even a comic strip) Aaron Hurst sets out a view of how purpose has become a central theme of the 21st century.

CHAPTER 2

From Command and Control to Align and Enable

Command and control has been the predominant leadership and management model for decades. Despite many and varied attempts to empower people, most managers revert to what they learned when they were starting out. Align and enable is an approach that is more fitting for today's circumstances.

Two types of organization need to get the best from people more than most: the military and late-stage start-ups. Both have developed leadership mindsets and approaches congruent with that need. And we can learn from them.

High performance in the military is critical from both a practical and a moral standpoint, particularly at a time when public resistance to war is on the rise.[14] And, in the world of a late-stage start-up, where cash is 'burned,' the need for a swift return on investment similarly demands a high-performance culture. Consequently, both kinds of organization have gone further than most in defining a leadership approach that delivers in a VUCA world (see *Chapter 1*).

What both kinds of organization understand is that people can't become high performers – acting quickly and decisively – in an overly controlled or constrained environment. Within a military environment, in which "no plan survives first contact with the enemy," responsiveness on the ground is critical. Command and control is not an option since the combatants will probably be out of contact with command and unable to wait for someone who is not familiar with developments on the ground to make a decision. Similarly, an effective start-up needs to be able to experiment, adjust and tweak in response to feedback, and iterate to create a new product or service quickly, unhampered by bureaucratic decision-making.

Both kinds of organization have had to resolve a specific problem: how can we empower people without losing focus and control?

In the US military, the solution to this problem lies in a philosophy called 'Mission Command.' And, in the world of high-growth start-ups, there is increasing clarity around what is sometimes referred to as the 'entrepreneurial mindset.'

Mission Command

As the 20th century ended and the 21st century began, the militaries of the developed nations found themselves facing a new challenge: battlefield environments had become far less predictable. Comparatively poorly resourced enemies, connected by modern technology, were able to confound the detailed planning of these better-trained armies.

Military strategists have long understood the advantage gained by allowing junior officers to exercise their initiative. Even so, it took the challenges of operating in the new world of the 21st century to make them re-evaluate the traditional command-and-control approach to leadership. In 2012 the US army published a white paper that explored the six principles of what it called Mission Command:[15]

- Build cohesive teams through mutual trust
- Create shared understanding
- Provide clear commander's intent
- Exercise disciplined initiative
- Use mission orders
- Accept prudent risk

These principles suggest that, in order to ensure success, understanding comes "from the bottom up and not just from the top down."[16] In other words, those in command become dependent on the understanding of their subordinates. Former US Navy submarine captain David Marquet argues that the historical method of passing information to those in authority is outdated and ineffective.[17] The role of those in senior positions is to delegate authority to those who hold the information. The role of the leader then changes from commander to enabler.

In this new thinking, the leader's job is to provide a clear vision of both the current state and the desired end state. Based on this vision, the leader then provides "mission-type orders."[18] These include a clear statement of intent and clarity on each unit's tasks in terms of the operational effects to be achieved. The leader does not provide orders regarding the precise execution of the tasks but trusts the skill and expertise of the people on the ground.

This culture of clarity and trust enables individual units and soldiers to use disciplined initiative within the boundaries of the leader's intent. Everybody accepts that risk is inevitable. While it should be managed and minimized, actions involving prudent levels of risk are acceptable. This understanding gives each unit, and each soldier, the freedom to act decisively within the operational intent.

Enabling this kind of autonomy and freeing individual teams and their members to act on their own initiative creates flexibility and the ability to adapt quickly in a way that traditional command structures cannot.

The entrepreneurial mindset

While we've learned a great deal from developments in military leadership, there is always a voice in the background that argues that business is not the military. Business teams are not the highly disciplined units you find in the military.

Leaders of high-growth start-ups also operate in fast-paced and challenging environments. Running a start-up is a race to deliver revenue before the initial capital runs out. In a similar way to their military counterparts, entrepreneurial leaders understand that a command-and-control approach is ineffective. They must believe in the ability of their team to use their skills, insight and expertise to deliver the desired business outcomes.

Effective entrepreneurial leaders set clear business objectives that are communicated to everyone involved. They ensure that each individual making up a team understands why they are doing their work. In this way, the entrepreneurial leader creates a clear context and direction for all the activity in the business. If an activity does not contribute to achieving the objective, then it is a distraction.

Having created clarity around the business objectives and direction of travel, entrepreneurial leaders recognize that their personal instinct to be in control of everything is potentially the biggest obstacle to achieving their goals. They recognize that the need for control creates a series of problems in a business:

- The leader becomes a bottleneck that slows progress and therefore costs money
- The business becomes constrained by the limited thinking of one person
- People become demotivated and feel undervalued

Entrepreneurial leaders understand that the people around them have skills, insights and expertise that are essential to the success of the business. They understand that to unlock this potential, they must believe in people's abilities to deliver the objectives of the business. To enable this, entrepreneurial leaders create a context in which teams, and the individuals within them, are trusted to take full responsibility for outcomes and act relentlessly until success is achieved.

Like their military counterparts, start-ups need to move quickly to use limited resources and time-constrained opportunities. They quickly obtain facts, get clarity on the decision that needs making and then act promptly. The only way to achieve this is to believe in the ability of the people in your team to use their skills, insights and expertise to deliver.

Similarities between Mission Command and entrepreneurial leadership

Mission Command and entrepreneurial leadership have some important similarities in the problems that they face:

- Both operate in fast-changing, complex environments with high levels of uncertainty
- Both need to act quickly, making the command-and-control approach too slow and inflexible
- Both need to maximize the performance of every individual

Unsurprisingly, the solutions to these problems – which have made a command-and-control culture increasingly ineffective in both military and business contexts – are also similar in their principles:

- Recognition of, and trust in, the capability of each individual member of the team
- The role of leadership to clearly communicate the business's vision and overarching goals, and the role of individuals and teams in achieving them
- The role of leadership in determining the desired outcomes
- Creating freedom for individuals and teams to determine what they need to do to achieve their objectives

In these models, the leader is less the commander and more the enabler. The role is less about wielding authority and more about distributing it. Success comes not from controlling activity but from creating a context where capable individuals can freely use their skills and insights to work together to achieve the desired outcomes.

If you have responsibility for the performance of other people, then it is your task to align and enable so that both they and the organization survive and thrive.

To align is to:

- Clarify *Why* the mission is important
- Clarify the context
- Clarify the overarching goals
- Align the overarching goals with the goals and projects of individuals
- Help team members align with and find meaning in the organization's mission and goals

To enable is to:

- Coach individual team members so that they have total clarity about how they will achieve their objectives
- Coach team members to achieve their objectives over time
- Ensure team members take responsibility and are accountable for achieving their objectives
- Give team members autonomy and authority to get on with their work
- Co-create development plans for the future

A THOUGHT EXPERIMENT TO TRY

Put yourself in the shoes of a member of your team:

- How would you respond to a constant flow of specific, detailed instructions?
- What would you need from your team leader in order to do your job well?
- As a team leader, what do you need to do differently?

WANT TO KNOW MORE?

"Understanding Mission Command" by Col. (Ret.) James D. Sharpe Jr and Lt. Col. (Ret.) Thomas E. Creviston[19]
An interesting article that sets out a brief history of Mission Command and the importance of trust in this model of leadership.

Turn the Ship Around! A True Story of Turning Followers into Leaders by David Marquet[20]
The story of how Captain David Marquet turned the worst-performing submarine crew in the US Navy into the best. You can apply his approach and create a workplace culture in which everyone takes responsibility for their actions.

Entrepreneurial Leadership: The Art of Launching New Ventures, Inspiring Others, and Running Stuff by Joel Peterson[21]
Joel Peterson lays out a path to becoming an entrepreneurial leader, with a series of leadership maps organized around what he calls the four essential base camps on the path to entrepreneurial leadership:

1. Establishing trust
2. Creating a sense of mission
3. Building a cohesive team
4. Executing and delivering results

CHAPTER 3

The Enabling Leader Model

Now that we understand that the role of a leader is to align and enable, how do we do that? What does it take to get your team to be the most effective and productive it can be? There are four key activities at which a team leader needs to be proficient.

The practical core of align and enable is the Enabling Leader model. This is a simple way of understanding your role and it will support you in building the habits and practices of a successful team leader.

The four activities of an enabling leader

The Enabling Leader model identifies four inter-related activities (as shown in *Figure 1*):

- **Relate**: every great team is built on the foundation of good relationships, and the first – essential – activity of anyone seeking to align and enable their team is to build and maintain effective relationships
- **Lead**: to provide context – to explain *why* the work is being done (Align)
- **Manage**: to communicate the practicalities – to explain *what* work needs to be done and *what* the business requires in terms of processes and procedures (Align)
- **Coach**: to work with your team to determine *how* the work will be done (Enable)

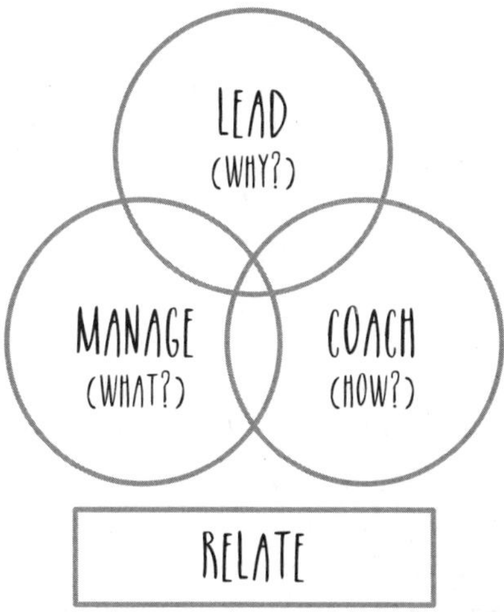

FIGURE 1 **THE ENABLING LEADER MODEL**

In later chapters we'll look at these four activities in more detail but for now here are the headlines.

LEAD: ALIGN TO THE *WHY*

The practices involved in ensuring that your team members understand *why* what they are doing is important are:

- Ensuring each team member understands what we might call the 'bigger picture': the overarching purpose and goals of the organization
- Ensuring each team member understands the context in which the organization is operating that make the overarching goals and purpose meaningful and significant
- Breaking down the organization's purpose and goals into the purpose and goals of the department or business unit in which the team member works

MANAGE: ALIGN TO THE *WHAT*

Explaining *what* each member of your team needs to do can only be done meaningfully when they have been aligned to the *Why*. The practices involved in ensuring each team member has complete clarity about *what* they need to do (and agrees to do it) are:

- Defining and agreeing the role of each team member
- Defining and agreeing individual goals and priorities
- Clarifying and agreeing how you will measure success and any quality standards and expectations
- Holding each team member to account for their achievements

COACH: ENABLING – THE *HOW*

Once again, this can only be done meaningfully when each team member has been aligned to the *Why* and the *What*. Once this has been achieved, your job becomes to enable them to bring their unique skills and insights to bear in deciding *how* the job is to be done. The practices involved are:

- Helping each team member think through their own approach or way forward

- Helping each team member solve their own problems as they progress
- Helping each team member take full responsibility for their task and actions

RELATE: THE ESSENTIAL FOUNDATION

All of the other elements rest on this. If there is a poor relationship, no meaningful conversations can take place, and you will not be able to lead, manage or coach. For a real conversation to happen, there needs to be trust. This is particularly true of a coaching conversation. Each member of your team must be able to talk about themselves, their role and how they go about it. They need freedom to talk openly about their strengths and desires as well as their failures and shortcomings.

When you focus on these four activities, you will see all of the benefits we have been speaking of:

- Team members will be more engaged and purposeful
- Team members, knowing the context, will make better decisions more quickly
- Team members will have a clear focus and a mandate
- Team members will understand the scope of their work and any constraints
- Team members will have greater ownership of their role, goals, decisions and actions
- Team members will learn and grow

In the following chapters, we will break down each of these activities – lead, manage, coach and relate – so that you can align and enable your team to be the best they can be.

Part of your task as a team leader is to enable the members of your team to get as close to their potential as they can. When you do that, both the business and the people in your team will thrive. Here's the extraordinary thing: when an individual team member knows *why* their work is important, has real clarity about *what* needs to be done and equally has clarity about *how* they are going to execute their tasks, many of the conditions required for high performance are met.

Tim Gallwey, author of the *Inner Game* series of books taught us a remarkably simple and profound idea:

Performance = Potential – Interference[22]

Tim's work asks and answers a very simple question: *what* stops people living up to their potential? He sums his answer up with the word 'interference' – the stuff that gets in the way. His suggestion is simple – the more you can reduce interference, the closer someone will get to living up to their potential. If a person is unclear about the *why*, is confused about the *what* and has no idea about the *how*, there is considerable interference and they can only fail. If you can help people identify and minimize the stuff that is interfering with them working to their potential, then their performance will inevitably improve.

The ultimate goal

Taking this idea one step further, one of the biggest studies of human beings and high performance was initiated by Mihaly Csikszentmihalyi, formerly professor of psychology and education at the University of Chicago. It was he who coined the term 'flow.'

Flow can be described as a state of "relaxed concentration" where there is minimal, or no, interference.[23] When you are in flow, you do what you do without the need for conscious thought. In that moment, everything else fades into the background – you are the master of your task and able to respond naturally to challenges.

Csikszentmihalyi identified what he called the conditions of flow. These might be summarized as follows:

- There are clear goals every step of the way
- There is immediate feedback to one's actions
- The individual has the skills required but is challenged by the activity
- Action and awareness are merged
- Distractions are excluded from consciousness
- There is no fear of failure
- Self-consciousness disappears
- The activity is its own reward

For some, flow is a profound and moving experience, very often coming when they are engaged in a physical activity. A friend of Myles used to race motorbikes and, occasionally, when he was absolutely at the limit, with his attention glued to the rider in front of him, he would get into his flow. His thoughts and actions would become one, time would seem to slow down, and the noise of the engines would appear to diminish. In this state, he would sense exactly when the rider in front was going to make a mistake and be able to capitalize on it without hesitation.

Being in flow does not have to be quite so dramatic. It can occur during such mundane activities as writing a report. You sit down at your desk and get started. You make a number of false starts; it is just not quite right. You get up, close the door, sit down and start again. Suddenly, the words begin to come. You become engrossed in the task. You look at your watch – an hour has gone by and you didn't even notice it. The report is half written.

Back in 2016, we had the privilege of working with Irena O'Brien, who is a cognitive neuroscientist who works out of Montreal in Canada. She was part of a team that put together a book called *Enabling Genius*. In the book Irena writes that, at work, flow "enhances people's creativity and productivity, corporate performance, and even shareholder value."[24] She also reviews various studies on how flow is experienced in the workplace. Among the benefits of this ultimate goal are:

- Improved customer loyalty
- Higher employee retention
- Higher sales
- Higher profit
- Higher levels of voluntary effort

As a team leader, it is worth setting yourself a goal to enable your team members and the team itself to spend more time in a deeper state of flow. But how do you go about aligning and enabling your team to be the best they can be and get the most satisfaction they can from their roles?

The Enabling Leader model gives you the tools you need to significantly reduce much of the interference that people experience in their work. And the core of this is to clarify and agree the *Why*, *What* and *How*.

A THOUGHT EXPERIMENT TO TRY

Think of a topic about which you need to talk with a member of your team. Break it down into the three domains of Lead – Manage – Coach.

- **Lead**: What is the big picture? How does this topic relate to the business's goals and objectives?
- **Manage**: What are the business's expectations? What do you need from the team and the individual team members?
- **Coach**: What scope is there to engage the team member to think through their approach?

WANT TO KNOW MORE?

The Inner Game of Work by Timothy Gallwey[25]
In this insightful book Timothy Gallwey applies his theories on performance to the world of work. A recommended read if you want to understand more about the interference that reduces our performance and how to reduce it.

Flow: The Psychology of Optimal Experience by Mihaly Csikszentmihalyi[26]
We've all used the phrase 'in the zone' to describe those moments when, without apparent effort, we achieve some of our best work. If you want to dig deeper into this 'Flow' state then this is the book for you.

The Advice Trap by Michael Bungay Stanier[27]
As those responsible for the performance of others, one of the biggest mistakes we can make is to fall into 'The Advice Trap.' Discover how to overcome your need to jump in with an idea or solution. Learn how to Tame your 'Advice Monster' and to enable your team members to come up with their own solutions.

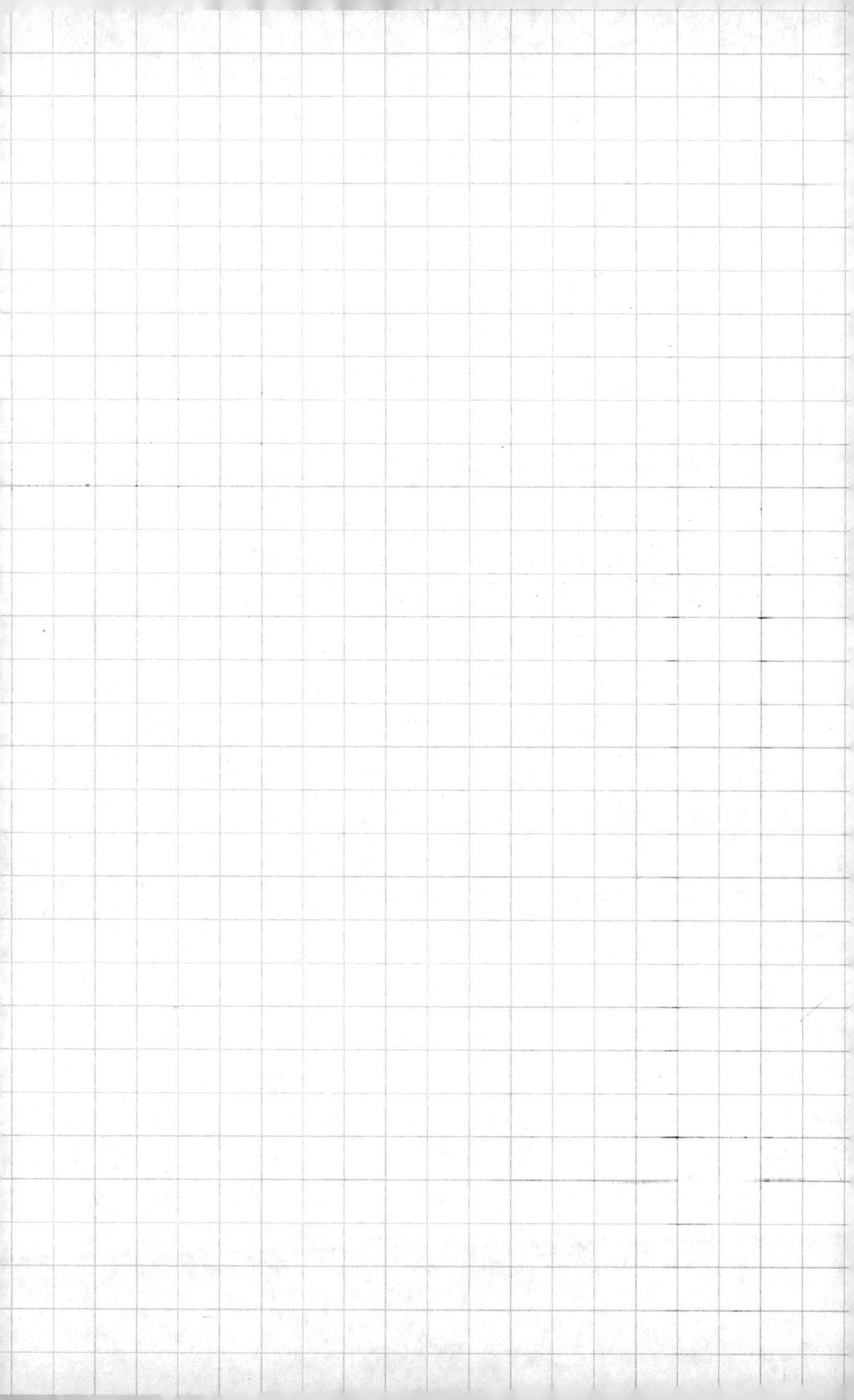

CHAPTER 4

Lead: Align with *Why*

We all work better when we understand *why* our work is valuable. Good team leaders provide a clear context for the work of their team.

The Enabling Leader model could be thought of as defining three types of conversation that will help you get the best out of other people. Lead – Manage – Coach is not an instruction to occupy three roles but a framework to help you think about the conversations you have with your colleagues, your direct reports and those to whom you are accountable.

Leadership is a skill set

The first thing to say is that, within our model, leadership is not a position or role. Leadership is a skill set. Your role may be defined as manager, team leader, section leader, supervisor or even CEO, but your role requires you to lead other people.

In the most effective teams, leadership moves around from person to person without resistance. That lack of resistance tells you something else about leadership – it is not about ego. Leadership is an act of service to the group. The role of the leader is to enable others to be the best they can be. When ego gets involved, people start defending their status as a leader and resisting the leadership of others in the team. A healthier view of leadership is described by Alan Keith of Genentech, who hit the nail on the head when he said that "leadership is ultimately about creating a way for people to contribute to making something extraordinary happen."[28]

The challenge in understanding leadership as a skill set (or function) rather than a role is that many leadership books approach the topic by describing the role of 'the leader.' Ask any group of people what they want from a leader and they will say 'vision' or 'direction.' The leader is seen as the one who shapes the vision and direction of the business. The trouble is that a healthy organization needs people to lead who do not have this level of influence.

ALIGNING WITH *WHY*

Leading is about providing context. It is about explaining *why* the work your team is doing is important and how it fits into the wider context of the business's objectives. People lead when they provide clarity around the mission and goals of the business and help others see how this is in some way meaningful. They lead when they motivate people by reminding them *why* they are doing the work and the difference they will make by doing it.

Leading doesn't necessarily require you to set the vision. It may be as simple as reminding people of the vision and finding ways to align it with individual team members' aspirations.

Here are some of the steps you can take to achieve this. Discuss with your team:

- Where are we now?
- Where do we need to be?
- When do we need to be there?
- Why do we want to get there?
- What difference will we make by achieving the desired outcomes?

Here is an idea of how this might work out in practice:

> Sophie is a brilliant asset to the team. She is full of innovative ideas that have the potential to unlock new and better ways of achieving the business's desired outcomes. The downside is that Sophie is full of innovative ideas about everything and her enthusiasm for her latest innovation can be as disruptive as it can be helpful.

One day, Sophie bounces up to your desk and asks if you have a few minutes to hear an idea she has had. You manage your initial reaction to being interrupted and choose to have the conversation, but you want to keep yourself, Sophie and the team focused on the current project. You say:

"Yes, of course I do. What's on your mind?"

Sophie shares her idea, but you are not immediately clear about how the idea contributes to the current objectives. You choose to put some boundaries around the conversation.

> "That sounds interesting. We're three weeks into the roll-out of the new stock control system, and I'm conscious that we are probably a couple of days behind where we wanted to be at this stage. We need to complete the roll-out by the end of next month."

Now you've created a context, you can re-engage with Sophie's idea:

> "I'd like to know more about your idea. Could you fill out some of the detail so that I understand how it would help with the roll-out?"

Sophie reflects that her idea probably doesn't change anything about the current project but explains the longer-term benefits to the business. Once again you provide some leadership:

> "Okay, it does sound interesting. Can I suggest that you take some time to capture your thoughts and then let's put aside some time to discuss your idea more fully toward the end of next month? And, Sophie, I really appreciate the way you are always looking at ways we can improve what we do."

In this short conversation, you have aligned Sophie's thinking with the needs of the business, kept the team on track and acknowledged the potential value of Sophie's idea in the longer term. Sophie feels valued and will capture her idea for future consideration before refocusing on delivering the new stock control system on schedule.

PASSION AND EXPERTISE

People lead most naturally when their passion or interest overlaps with their responsibility to deliver. We've all seen it: the person in the room who hasn't said much suddenly comes alive when the team starts talking about their 'thing' – the topic, issue or area of expertise that animates them.

Handled badly, your 'thing' becomes a soapbox or a drum you bang. If you act like your 'thing' is the only 'thing' that matters, you'll steer your team down a blind alley or just annoy them. On the other hand, when your 'thing' is relevant, your passion and expertise will motivate and inspire the people around you. The same is true of your team members: you need to make space for their 'thing' to shine when it can contribute the most.

That same passion and expertise, used in the service of the team, will create trust – your intent is clear and transparent. As we have said, without a trusting relationship, your colleagues will not allow you to provide context and direction for their work. Your ability to harness your passion and expertise in their service is a significant part of building that trusting relationship.

A THOUGHT EXPERIMENT TO TRY

Write down the key business objectives of your team. Choose the one that most interests you.

- How would you describe where you are now in relations to the goal?
- What makes this objective important for the business?
- What difference will your team make by successfully achieving this objective?

Your answers could form a framework for the Lead part of the conversations you need to have with your team.

WANT TO KNOW MORE?

Start with Why by Simon Sinek[29]

This classic book by Simon Sinek explores why some people and organizations are more inventive, pioneering and successful than others, and why they are able to repeat their success again and again. The answer is that in business it doesn't matter what you do, it matters *why* you do it. This is a simple way of thinking about what motivates the people in your team.

The Purpose Effect by Dan Pontefract[30]

In this insightful book, Dan Pontefract explores the benefits to be gained when our personal sense of purpose connects with the purpose of the organization in which we work.

Wave Rider by Harrison Owen[31]

Wave Rider explores the art of enabling high performance by creating a context in which teams self-organize.

CHAPTER 5

Manage:
Align with *What*

Effective team leaders understand that what a team member does must align with and contribute to the overarching business objectives. At the same time, leaders must ensure there is total clarity about what's expected in terms of performance.

At the bottom left of the Enabling Leader model is a circle we labelled 'Manage' (see *Figure 2*). Once again this is not about having the status, or label, of being a manager. It is a type of conversation that is needed to get the best out of others. In the previous chapter we described leading as providing context that aligns people's objectives with the direction of the business. To manage is to align what your team is doing with the overarching business goals.

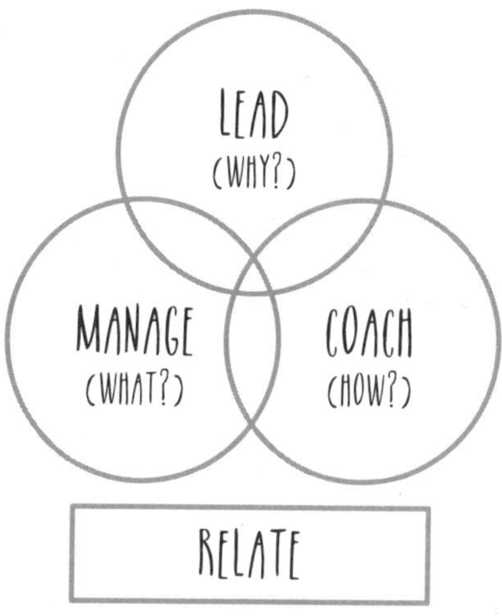

FIGURE 2 **A REMINDER OF THE ENABLING LEADER MODEL**

Objectives and Key Results

Objectives and Key Results (OKR) is a model that was developed by Intel in the 1970s.[32] The model involves a very simple three-step process:

- The business sets objectives and identifies the key results for those objectives (this is often done for each year and each quarter)
- Each team sets objectives and identifies its own key results that are aligned with the business objectives
- Team leaders work with individual team members to identify individual objectives and key results aligned with the team and business objectives

Part of your job as a team leader is to align the activities of your team, and the individuals within it, to the business objectives. Manage-style conversations break down that intent into departmental and individual goals and tasks and keep people on track.
The Manage conversation is concerned with practicalities:

- Deadlines
- Team and individual objectives
- Projects and tasks
- Standards
- Processes and procedures
- Resources

The importance of these practicalities can be seen to play out in every public park. If you watch a group playing football at your local park, you'll notice that it will usually begin with four sweatshirts or coats being placed as goal posts and an assumption that this is enough.

The game then quickly breaks down into one (or both) of two arguments:

- The ball passes high between the 'posts' and is pronounced (by the defending team) to have gone over a non-existent crossbar – the goal wasn't defined well enough
- In midfield, the play gets wider and wider until someone proclaims that the ball 'must' be out of play – the boundaries were not defined well enough

Unless the group can agree boundaries, the game is unplayable.

On a sports field, the lines on the ground provide boundaries that make the game playable. Beyond the outer lines, the ball is out of play. In football, the penalty box defines the area in which the goalkeeper can handle the ball and within which a foul may lead to a penalty. The centre line ensures a fair start, with everyone on their own side. The corner markings define the area within which the ball must be placed for a corner kick.

The lines make the game playable by ensuring that everyone knows when a goal is achieved and the boundaries within which the rules apply. These boundaries and rules are not there to limit the game but to enable it to be played fairly and efficiently.

Management is the skill of drawing the lines that enable the team to play the game fairly and efficiently.

We can push the football analogy further (apologies to the non-football-fans – the analogy works with other sports too). The manager is also the person who makes sure the players are in the right part of the field and fulfilling the right tasks at the right time in the game.

Managing the overlaps

Looking again at the Enabling Leader model, you will notice that Lead and Manage overlap with each other and with Coach. What this represents is that, in one conversation – and potentially in a single sentence – you can move from Lead to Manage, or vice versa. Similarly, both Lead and Manage conversations can quickly turn into opportunities for a Coach conversation, and vice versa.

Let's return to Sophie, from *Chapter 4*.

Imagine, after your last conversation with Sophie, you notice that she has become fixated on her idea and it is affecting her productivity. Now you need a different kind of conversation with her. You say:

> "Sophie, I just wanted to follow up on the conversation we had about your idea. Have you managed to capture it somewhere?"

She says that she has put it on Evernote and she still thinks it could be great. In fact, she has been giving it a lot of thought and has some suggestions on how to develop her idea that she would like to share when you have time. You say:

> "We did say we would set aside some time to talk at the end of next month. Let's get something in the diary now."

You agree a time and date. You say:

> "I'm conscious that this idea has really captivated you and I need you to give your full attention to the current project. How are you getting on with the stuff you need to deliver?"

Sophie says she is doing okay. You ask a few more questions and she admits that she is falling behind. You move into a brief coaching conversation to help her understand what is causing her to be behind and, among other things, she admits that she has been preoccupied with her idea. You say:

> "It is a great idea and I'm looking forward to chatting about it next month. For now, I need you to focus on the task at hand and to meet your deadlines. If you don't, it will affect the whole team. What could you do to regain your focus?"

You have realigned Sophie with her tasks and made sure she will play her part in delivering the current project. You end by moving into a coaching conversation that enables her to own the actions that will refocus her activity onto fulfilling her responsibility to the team.

In Lead – Manage – Coach, the Manage conversation is focused on ensuring that the work people do contributes to the business goals and is aligned to the practicalities of the business. Finally, it ensures that they have all the resources they need to do the job.

A THOUGHT EXPERIMENT TO TRY

Identify a team member in whom you see room for improvement. Consider the following questions:

- What, in your mind, are the key improvements they need to make?
- What is the conversation you could have with them?

WANT TO KNOW MORE?

Build It: The Rebel Playbook for World-Class Employee Engagement by Glenn Elliott and Debra Corey[33]
At the heart of this book is a valuable model that breaks down the contributing factors of employee-engagement. The authors take a radically people-centred approach that is full of useful ideas for those wanting to build a business culture in which people thrive.

Measure What Matters by John Doerr[34]
For those wanting to find out more about using Objectives and Key Results, this book is full of useful insights backed up with first-person case studies.

CHAPTER 6

Coach: Enable – the *How*

Effective team leaders use coaching skills to enable their teams to engage with their work and deliver their objectives, in a way that unlocks the potential of the team and the individuals within it.

When we talk about the Enabling Leader model with managers and leaders, there is one question that comes up again and again. People can quickly understand the value of conversations that fall into the Lead or Manage parts of the model. But coaching? That's not my job. That's for HR. It's for people who are failing!

In 2017, Myles worked with the senior coaches to the English national rugby team. They saw, and see, coaching as a means of drawing the best performance out of the players. It's not for people who are failing – it's for people who are performing!

We are not suggesting you become a coach. What we are saying is that there is a type of conversation that uses coaching skills that is essential in helping your team to be productive, effective and engaged.

Coaching conversations

Let's start with two definitions that you can find in Myles's book *Effective Modern Coaching*. The first originated with The School of Coaching:

> *Coaching is the art of facilitating the performance, learning and development of another.*[35]

Let's break it down. In the context of a business, coaching is ultimately concerned with *performance*. That may relate to the execution of a specific task or project, the achievement of business goals, or (more generically) greater effectiveness or efficiency. A business may also use coaching skills to enable *learning*. This is as important as performance because, taking a longer-term view, the future performance of the business depends on it. Finally, a business can use coaching skills to enable someone's *development* (i.e. personal growth and greater self-awareness) in order for them to discover greater levels of effectiveness.

Once you isolate those words – performance, learning and development – you can see how coaching skills fit within your role as a team leader. It is almost the definition of your role:

- To enable better performance
- To enable your team to learn skills and gain understanding that will improve their work
- To enable the kind of personal growth and self-awareness that are key to teams functioning well

We are aware that the word 'coaching' is commonly used much more broadly. It is used to describe anything from the passing on of expert knowledge to therapy. The key to cutting through all this confusion is to define coaching by its outputs. And in business that means enabling the people in our teams to perform at the top end of their potential.

So, coaching is the art of facilitating: of enabling someone to think something through for themselves; to have an insight or creative idea. When you coach, your role is to enable a member of your team to explore something for themselves: to gain a better understanding, to become more aware, and from that place to make a better decision than they would have made on their own.

The second definition is from *Effective Modern Coaching*:

> Effective coaching in the workplace delivers achievement, fulfilment and joy from which both the individual and the organization benefit.[36]

When coaching is *effective* in the workplace it delivers *achievement*. It delivers extraordinary results: organizational and individual goals are achieved; strategies, projects and plans are executed. Once again, this could almost be your job description as a team leader.

Then comes the magic. When you use coaching as a tool to deliver these achievements, you also deliver *fulfilment* and *joy*. The people involved learn and grow, and find their work more engaging, fulfilling and enjoyable. By choosing to coach, you demonstrate trust and respect for your team. You also give them the chance to use their knowledge, skills and insights. They are more involved, feel valued and, as a result, become more committed to the success of the team and the business. Everyone benefits.

Probably the most important distinction between Lead and Manage, on the one hand, and Coach, on the other, is that in a coaching conversation, the intent is to enable the other person to think for themselves.

We've all seen pictures and comics where a thought bubble appears over a character's head to reveal what they are thinking. A great coach and former colleague used to ask, "Over whose head is the thought bubble?" Ideally, the thought bubble should be over the head of the person being coached (see *Figure 3*). They do the thinking, not the person doing the coaching. This is probably the simplest way we have to communicate what effective coaching is about.

FIGURE 3 **OVER WHOSE HEAD IS THE THOUGHT BUBBLE?**

Directive coaching vs following interest

When you are in Coach mode, your job is to create an environment where the team member can do their very best thinking. This is different from traditional approaches to coaching, where the coach is doing the thinking, making decisions and solving problems. This brings us to a key distinction between directive and non-directive coaching. 'Non-directive' is a clumsy phrase – it tells you what not to do, not what to do. So, we will refer to 'following interest' instead of non-directive and stick with 'directive.' Let us describe them.

Figure 4 lays out most of the conversational approaches you might take as a team leader when coaching, organized in a spectrum from directing to following interest.

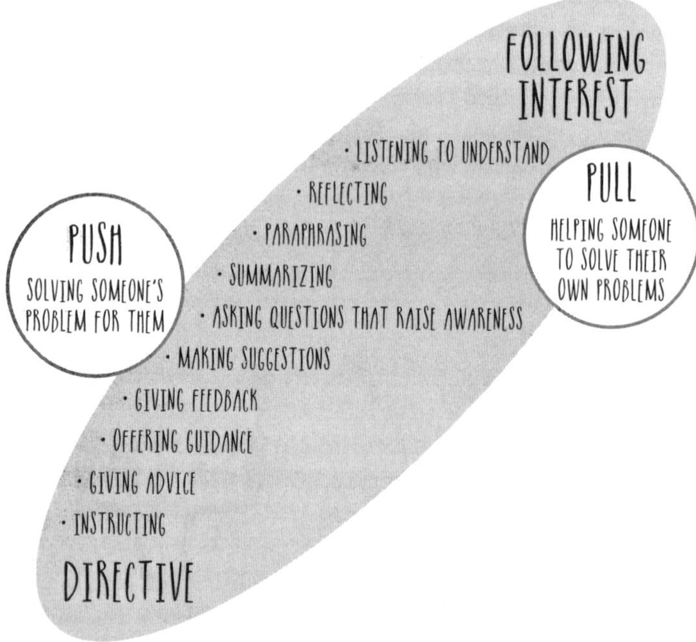

FIGURE 4 **THE SPECTRUM OF CONVERSATIONAL SKILLS**

Directing means just that: to direct, to tell or to instruct. It is the form of education and management that we are most familiar with. The directive skills are available to you as a coach, but the greatest impact is made by facilitating and following interest.

Occasionally, as part of a training programme to develop coaching skills, we take the participants onto a tennis court. The purpose is to get them to deepen their facilitation skills by following interest, the theory being that if they do not know the techniques involved in playing tennis, they cannot resort to instructions.

What is baffling is that participants who have never played tennis before will still try to tell others how to play! It seems that we are so used to being told what to do, and to telling others what to do, that frequently we do not see that teaching has little to do with learning.

What is amazing – and it amazes us every time we see it – is the results that participants achieve when they adopt an approach based on Following Interest. People learn in minutes things that would take a traditional coach, operating from a more conventional model, hours to teach. (Or, rather, minutes to teach – but forever to get across!)

In following interest you do not direct, instruct or tell. Think about how you learned to walk. You learned to walk through direct experience – a kind of trial and error. You stood up and you had a go. You fell over. You unconsciously processed the information gained from that experience, took account of the results and made the appropriate corrections. Most of us walk reasonably well, but few have had any direct instruction in how to do it.

Think about what did *not* happen when you learned to walk. A willing parent did not stand behind you, armed with *The Parenting Book that Has Been Handed Down through the Ages*, and issue a series of instructions: "Great – now put all your weight on your right leg.

Okay. Let your left leg swing forward. Try to get some balance with your arms – no, stupid, your left leg!" (You get the picture!)

Nor were there recriminations, punishments or blame when you got it wrong. Parents in the early days are blessed with a non-judgemental approach that encourages experimentation and playfulness. And then, somewhere along the way, we – as parents, teachers and team leaders – forget this.

So here's the key: each one of us is born with an innate capacity to learn – a sort of learning instinct, if you will. An effective team leader seeks to tap into that instinct to enable other people to learn for themselves. We'll describe exactly how in the next two chapters.

Despite the limitations of a directive or 'tell' approach, it is important to understand that the directive end of the spectrum is also available to you. There will be times when you *do* know the answer and the other person is stuck. There will be times when the other person needs some feedback or advice. In these situations, to withhold an answer would not be helpful. However, the real breakthroughs and moments of genius emerge from the other end of the spectrum.

Once they have given some thought to *why* their team members are engaged in the work they do and *what* their team members need to achieve, most managers find it relatively easy to have Lead- or Manage-style conversations. The challenge comes with Coach. Facilitating non-directive conversations – following interest – and knowing when to move back toward the directive end of the spectrum requires a specific skill set that few people develop naturally. For this reason, the next few chapters will focus on these skills. In the end, it is these coaching skills that unlock the power of the Enabling Leader model.

A THOUGHT EXPERIMENT TO TRY

Think of a time when you were playing a sport or doing a job but things were not working out well. What was going on inside your head? Did it help?

Now think of a time when you were in the zone – a time when you were at your best and you were enjoying every moment. What was going on inside your head?

Think of a time at work when you were facing a task you felt was outside your skill set. What did you need from the person leading that activity?

Think of a time when you were confident and felt like your work was exactly what you signed up for. How would you have liked someone to support you in this situation?

WANT TO KNOW MORE?

Effective Modern Coaching by Myles Downey[37]
Myles' first book, now in its third edition, has become a key text for those interested in developing coaching skills.

Dialogue: The Art of Thinking Together by William Isaacs[38]
A great book that provides a practical approach to creating truly collaborative thinking. For a deep dive into the art of successful dialogue, this is a great read.

CHAPTER 7

‘Coach’: The Models

There are two key models you can use to structure your conversations with your team. These will align them with the needs of the business and enable them to bring their insights, skills and creativity to the table.

In the previous chapter, we saw how enabling others to think for themselves in a focused way can deliver achievement, fulfilment and joy, from which both the individual and the organization will benefit.

In this chapter we will look at two models that can help to structure your conversations to ensure you see these results.

The GROW model

The GROW model is a useful framework even when the whole conversation only lasts five minutes (see *Figure 5*).

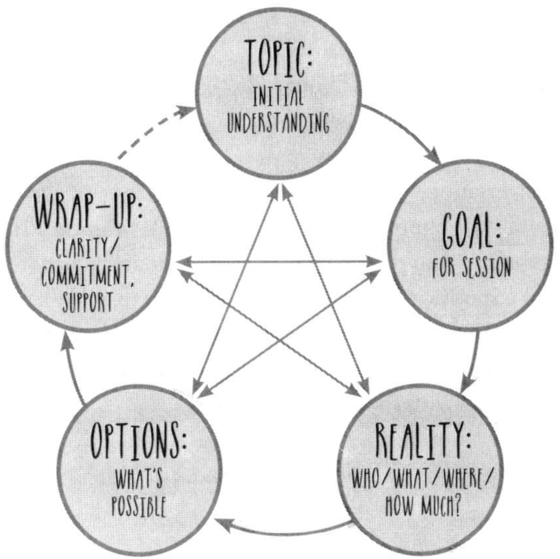

FIGURE 5 **THE GROW MODEL**

The first time you use the GROW model, it can feel unnatural but once you have used it a few times, it begins to feel fluent, to the point where you hardly have to think about it, or you refer to it only as a sort of checking-in point if the conversation is not going well.

The first letter of each stage in the model gives you GROW. Well, almost. What is missing is the first and rather critical stage: that of identifying the topic for the conversation. For this reason, some people refer to it as the T-GROW model.

The strength of this model is that it grew out of best practice. Over time, it became apparent that in the more successful coaching conversations there was a certain sequence of key stages, and it is these key stages that are captured in the model. Imagine someone comes to you and you decide that the most appropriate conversation would be a coaching conversation. The natural sequence of questions you would ask might go something like this:

- "What do you want to talk to me about?"
- "What's actually happening?"
- "What could you do about it?"
- "What are you definitely going to do about it?"

In this conversation, you would have covered four of the five elements of GROW: topic, reality, options and wrap-up. The only element missing from the perspective of the model is that you never established a specific goal for your conversation (e.g. "What do you need to get out of this conversation?"). Adding that one missing element could introduce a level of focus that ensures the actions agreed are in line with the desired outcome.

Let's look at each stage of the GROW model in more detail.

TOPIC

This is the first stage in any coaching conversation. At this point, a detailed account of the subject matter is not necessary. What you want is to understand the territory you are in, the scale of the topic, the importance and sometimes the emotional significance for the other person. It is sometimes useful to establish what your team member's longer-term vision or goal is. You are looking for that moment when something inside you says: "*This* is what they want to talk about."

At the topic stage, your intention is to understand what, specifically, the other person wants to talk about. Following is an example.

Team leader (TL): What would you like to talk about?

Team member (TM): As you know, I've got to make a presentation to the board next week, and I'm a bit nervous about doing a good job.

TL: Tell me some more about that.

TM: The team have asked me to make the presentation on Project Blue, and I am not at all sure how I should approach it.

TL: Right.

TM: And to tell the truth, I'm a bit nervous about standing up before the board. They have a reputation for being tough on people who don't present well.

TL: Yes, I know. Is there anything else?

TM: Not really. (*then, after a pause*) Well, yes, the last time I made a presentation to a senior group it did not go very well.

TL: Let me check. Is there a broader issue here about your presentation skills?

TM: I guess so.

TL: Specifically, then, what is it you want to talk about?

TM: It's about making a good presentation to the board, and also about improving my presentation skills in general.

TL: If you could make progress with those skills, how would you want it to be?

GOAL

While all the stages of the GROW model are critical, the goal stage has perhaps the greatest impact on the success of the conversation. In fact, 'goal' is not the best word to describe this stage. The coach is trying to establish the desired *outcome* for the conversation – something that will be achieved within the discussion itself. The 'goal' is not the longer-term objective that the other person has for the topic.

For example, a goal or vision to generate £400,000 of new sales in the next three months cannot be achieved in a single conversation. The outcome of the conversation might be to have a *strategy* to deliver £400,000 of new sales in the next three months.

When you are clear about the outcome, you have a focus for the conversation. Together with the other person, you have defined an achievable outcome for your conversation. You can keep the conversation focused on this outcome and you will both know when you have achieved it.

Team leader (TL): Okay, I think I've got a fair understanding of the topic. Tell me what you would like to get out of this conversation.

Team member (TM): Well, I'm more concerned about the immediate problem – the presentation to the board, than I am about meeting the longer-term target. So, I'd like to focus more on that.

TL: Fine. And tell me what else you want from this conversation.

TM: Well, I'd like to understand what went wrong in the presentation to the senior managers that I mentioned, and then to have an idea of the key things to do differently next week.

TL: There are two parts to that: to understand what went wrong and to have an idea of the key things to do differently. Take the first part. What outcome would you want from understanding what went wrong?

TM: To have identified the key lessons.

TL: What does 'key' mean?

TM: The most important. The two or three things that make or break a presentation.

TL: And for the second part? "The key things to do differently." What outcome would you like from that?

TM: Obviously, the discussion about what went wrong may give me some of the things to do differently, but I suspect there are some other things that I need to know.

TL: And the outcome?

TM: If I could find five or six key things to do or remember, that would be great.

REALITY

This stage of the GROW model is concerned with achieving the most accurate picture of the topic possible. Your role is to encourage the other person to discuss and become more aware of all aspects of the topic. In this phase, your primary function is to understand: not to solve, fix, heal, make better or be wise, but to *understand*. No analysis, no problem solving, no wisdom, no good ideas, no jumping to conclusions. The magic is that in the moment you understand the other person, they will become more aware and understand for themselves – and are then in a position to make better decisions and choices than they would have made without you.

At this stage, your intention is to generate the clearest possible understanding of the topic.

Team leader (TL): You've mentioned the presentation that didn't work so well and then this other, more generic, "other things you might do." Are there any other elements to this?

Team member (TM): Not that I can think of.

TL: Which of the two do you want to tackle first?

TM: I think the obvious place to start is with the presentation that I messed up.

TL: Okay. Tell me about that.

TM: It was in an earlier stage of this project. I thought it was going to be relatively straightforward, but in the event it turned out all wrong.

TL: Just how bad was it?

TM: It wasn't a complete disaster, and they did get the message. It was that I really didn't do the work we had done – or myself – justice.

TL: So, what actually happened?

TM: I was a bit flustered when I got there. We had worked late the night before, and at that point I thought I knew what I had to do. However, on the morning I felt unprepared. I was still putting the slides in order minutes before I was due to start.

TL: What else happened?

TM: Apart from not feeling prepared, I was really nervous, and my words came out a bit scrambled. At one point, someone asked me to repeat what I had just said because they had not understood.

TL: Was there anything else in the session that did not work for you?

TM: Yes. I was put out by a number of the questions. I don't think that anyone was trying to be difficult – I just found it tricky to find the answers.

TL: So far in this conversation, you've mentioned something about your preparation, about feeling nervous and the difficulty you had in answering questions. Is there anything else that you remember?

TM: Not really. That's enough to work with.

OPTIONS

Once the clearest possible understanding of the situation or topic has been reached, the discussion naturally turns to what can be done – to what it is possible for the other person to do. We use 'possible' – as in 'that's a possibility' – in the biggest, most creative sense, rather than in a narrow, restrictive one. In the reality phase, a clear understanding is gained, and it is from this understanding that the possibilities emerge.

The intention here is to draw out a list of all that is possible without judgement or evaluation.

Team leader (TL): We've spoken about preparation, nervousness and handling questions in some depth now. In looking to move forward, which of those would you like to pursue first?

Team member (TM): I still think there is most mileage in the 'handling questions' bit. If I can get that right, it will help with the nervousness issue, and the preparation bit should be easy to crack.

TL: Where we got to with handling questions, as I understood you, was that you felt that you had not always fully understood the question.

TM: Yes, and that was partly because I was thinking of my next slide.

TL: So, what could you do differently?

TM I could make sure that no questions were asked until the end of the session.

TL: What else?

TM: I could just stop myself from going to the next slide – maybe make eye contact. That would help.

TL: Anything else?

TM: Not sure.... Well, if I haven't heard I could ask the questioner to repeat the question, or if I think I've heard but I'm not sure, I suppose I could check my understanding by repeating the question.

TL: What else can you think of?

WRAP-UP

This is the final stage of the GROW model, with lots of options on the table. What remains is to select the most appropriate and agree the next steps. It is often useful to check the other person's commitment to the chosen course of action and to see if any support is required. It is almost always useful to get them to say exactly what their action plan is. If they state the action plan, it ensures clarity and agreement – and, from the tone of voice, you can ascertain their level of commitment.

At this stage, the intention is to gain commitment to action.

Team leader (TL): Of all the options that we have identified, which ones do you think you might action?

Team member (TM): I can't remember them all.

TL: I think I jotted most of them. There are those options that came out of the discussion about the presentation, concerning preparation, nervousness and handling questions. Then there were the options that came out of the second part of the discussion. Where do you want to start?

TM: Let's start with the handling questions bit.

TL: You came up with four options: keeping the questions to the end of the session, stopping and making eye contact, asking the questioner to repeat the question, and playing your understanding of the question back.

TM: That's right. The only one I'm uncomfortable about is the first one: keeping questions until the end.

TL: What is it that makes you uncomfortable?

TM: Despite the fact that I'm not very good at it, I do want to keep the sessions as interactive as possible. So, I think I'll skip that one. The others I can do.

TL: Just so we are both sure, tell me specifically what you are going to do?

TM: In the presentation to the board, when I hear a question, I will stop thinking of what I have to do next and make eye contact with the questioner. If I don't hear the question fully, I will either ask the person to repeat it or, if I've got the gist of it, I will check my understanding by playing it back.

TL: Okay. Now which part do you want to tackle next?

THE GROW MODEL: A SUMMARY

The following analogy is not watertight, but it should make what we have said even clearer. When the other person begins to talk, it is most likely that their thoughts about the topic will be unclear and jumbled up. It's a bit like a jigsaw puzzle, only in this case the pieces are in a bag and there is no cover picture to act as a guide. As they talk, the corner pieces and some of the edges are identified and put on the table. The scale and the nature of the topic thus become a little clearer. At this point, it is possible to set a goal (outcome), as you both know exactly what you are discussing, even if all the details are not yet clear. Moving on to the reality phase, you encourage the other person to put all the pieces of the jigsaw – or all they are aware of – on the table.

As the conversation progresses, the other person will notice that some of the pieces are face down and others are in the wrong place. When most of the pieces are turned face up and shuffled into the right places, a picture or pattern emerges. At this point, the other person is seeing the whole picture, and they will find new insight, come to a solution or a possible option. From this point onward, the other person can usually begin to make some choices about the next steps.

The GROW model is shown in *Figure 5* as a circle because in the most straightforward conversations you move from topic to goal to reality to options to wrap-up and then maybe agree a time and a place for the next conversation. However, the arrows between the stages reflect the fact that not all conversations are straightforward, and you may have to shuffle between the stages. For instance, in the wrap-up stage the other person may identify a new option, or in the reality stage it may become clear that the goal is not appropriate. If this happens, simply return to the relevant part of the model. Do not get stuck in its linear nature – few people think in a strictly linear fashion, and it is your job to follow their interest (see *Chapter 6*).

The Model T

As we have said, when you choose to coach, your role is to encourage members of your team to think, but not to think for them. You need to stay on *their* agenda and to follow *their* interest. This is not an easy thing to do at first, because your instinct will likely be to think about the issue and try to solve it. What we have noticed over the years is that when we suggest that an instinctive response will not help the other person, many team leaders in training are at a loss as to what to do instead.

This is where the Model T – so named because of the way it is presented diagrammatically – comes in. The Model T is a remarkably powerful technique for making progress in the GROW model, as it is the structure behind the idea of following interest. It suggests that you expand the conversation first, then focus on the detail (see *Figure 6*).

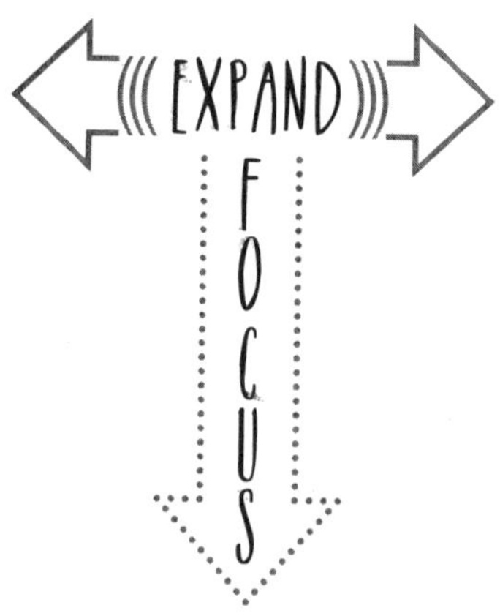

FIGURE 6 **THE MODEL T**

Imagine that you are in the options stage of the GROW model. The conversation might go like this:

Team leader (TL): You've given me one option: to delegate the project to Jamie. What other options are there? (*Expanding*)

Team member (TM): I could give it to Jamie but still supervise it myself.

TL: Anything else? (*Expanding again*)
TM: I could do it myself.
TL: Anything else?
TM: I can't think of anything.
TL: Okay. But let's see if there are any other options. Tell me what you would really like to do, regardless of consequences? (*Expanding again – and adding a little creativity*)
TM: Well, what I'd really like is not to do it at all. But that's not realistic. Having said that, I could delay it for a couple of weeks until I'm less busy.
TL: So, four options then: hand it to Jamie completely, hand it to Jamie and you supervise, do it yourself, and delay it until later. Which of those is most interesting? (*Focusing and leaving choice and responsibility with the team member*)

The Model T has some inherent benefits. Often, the temptation is to seek a resolution as quickly as possible. There are many dangers in this, not least that, in an attempt to make progress, information that might be relevant is omitted. The Model T keeps you on the other person's agenda, and because it suggests that you expand the conversation before going into detail, most, if not all, of the relevant information is picked up.

The model should also be used in the topic and reality phases. If the person you are talking with describes a particular aspect of an issue and you ask them to tell you more about it (*focusing*), there is the possibility that time will be invested in discussing something that is not entirely relevant to the overall issue. Far better is to ask whether there is anything else (*expanding*) and then, having heard any other aspects of the issue, to focus on the aspect that appears to be most relevant.

Team leader (TL): So, you've told me that the project is behind and that you're going to miss the next milestone, and you've also mentioned the poor performance of your team. Is there anything else? (*Summarizing, then expanding*)

Team member (TM): We have an internal client, a sponsor from the board, who is also slowing things down.

TL: The project, the team and the sponsor. Which is most interesting to discuss first? (*Focusing*)

TM: Actually, we should really talk about the sponsor. When we started the conversation, I thought it was really all about the poor performance of the team, but without a clear remit from our sponsor, it is always going to be difficult to be successful.

In this snippet of conversation, you can see that, if the team leader had not *expanded* the conversation, the issue of the internal sponsor might have been overlooked. Notice also the way the team leader used the word 'interesting' in the *focusing* question.

Initially, this surprises people – they expect words like 'relevant' or 'important.' If the team leader had used the word 'important' instead, there is a possibility that it might have generated interference (see *Chapter 3*) and pushed the team member into trying to find 'the right answer.' The team member might well have become less relaxed as they tried to make the 'right' choice in a matter that the team leader had indicated was 'important.' It's far better to follow interest, as there is less danger of judgement. Interest allows room for intuition and feelings, among other things, and will almost always generate a richer conversation.

There is another helpful way to describe this. We call it Floodlight and Spotlight. Floodlight comes first, shedding light on the whole territory and into every nook and cranny. Then comes the spotlight, which brings light to a specific aspect – chosen, most often, by the team member, following interest. Of course, the team leader can also direct the other person's attention, and we will address that later, in *Chapter 10*, under 'Proposing.'

A THOUGHT EXPERIMENT TO TRY

Find a piece of paper and work through this exercise:

1. Think of a topic that is currently occupying your attention.
2. How would you explain it to someone else?
3. What else could you tell them about this topic?
4. What outcome would you like from this exercise?
5. What else would someone need to know to understand the issue?
6. How would you like the issue to be?
7. What could you do to move the issue forward?
8. What else could you do?
9. If there were no constraints, what would you really like to do to move the issue forward?
10. What are you going to do?
11. What is your next step?

WANT TO KNOW MORE?

Coaching for Performance by John Whitmore[39]

If you want to take a deeper dive into the GROW model, then John Whitmore's classic book is a great place to start. Highly recommended if you want to develop your understanding of coaching.

CHAPTER 8

Three Essential Coaching Skills

Within our approach to coaching, three skills are arguably more important than any others, in terms of the impact on team members. These are following interest, raising awareness and listening to understand. Following interest was addressed in *Chapters 6* and *7* but underpins this chapter too. This chapter considers the other two skills.

Raising awareness

Myles grew up in a time when it was possible to fix your own car. The first time he looked under the bonnet he saw a mass of metal, with pipes, hoses and wiring. Because he did not understand what he was seeing, he was powerless to fix the car or make any improvements to its performance. As he began to understand the function of the various parts and the relationships between them – as his awareness was raised – he became powerful, at least in the context of that particular car. He could then make repairs and improvements.

Here's an example of what raising awareness looks like in the workplace. To change things up, rather than a conversation between team leader and team member, this shows two colleagues in an informal conversation: coaching can be used in many different ways.

Linda: Hi, Tom, how are you?
Tom: Not so good, really!
Linda: What's up?
Tom: I'm in the middle of an emergency sales meeting and we've just taken a break. It's going horribly wrong.
Linda: In what way is it going wrong?
Tom: We're way behind on the agenda and Paul and Tiana are at each other's throats, again!
Linda: Anything else?
Tom: Maybe. The atmosphere is a bit strange.
Linda: Of those three things – the agenda, Paul and Tiana, and the atmosphere – which is most interesting to talk about?
Tom: The atmosphere. It's not just Paul and Tiana. The others are acting up too.
Linda: Acting up?
Tom: Yes. Snapping at each other, complaining, not listening to each other.
Linda: So, what can you do?

Tom: We have to talk about it, it's so out of character. I could start by giving them feedback, tell them what I'm noticing and then ask them what they think.

Linda: Great. Will that be enough?

Tom: Yes. Once it's brought to their attention, we'll either find out what's going on, if anything, or just behave better – we're all tired and stressed. Thanks!

Some years ago, Myles saw Tim Gallwey (see *Chapter 3*) work briefly with a senior management consultant in one of the 'big five' accountancy practices. He had a problem with anxiety when faced with very senior clients, such as CEOs. The conversation went something like this.

Tim Gallwey (TG): How anxious do you get, say on a scale of one to ten?

Management consultant (MC): About seven or eight.

TG: Will you be meeting anyone with whom you might get anxious in the next few weeks?

MC: Yes. (*The management consultant gave details of two or three such meetings.*)

TG: What I suggest is that you rate your anxiety on a scale of one to ten just before, during and after the meetings.

End of conversation. In Tim's words, "awareness is curative."[40] Simply noticing something is enough for your brain to work on improving it.

Noticing is a key part of becoming aware. It is without judgement and is untainted by fear, doubt, aspiration or wish. Noticing is the 'not trying' of thinking. It allows us to take in a much broader band and quantity of data, and, as there is no judgement, eliminates interference (see *Chapter 3*). We then process this data in a way that effortlessly and elegantly produces results that are often surprising.

Imagine being in a conversation with someone from your team. They are responsible for the relationship with one of your best clients and have made a poor decision that has led to a hiccup in the relationship. They need to understand how to recover and move forward. Instead of jumping in to save the day, you decide to help them understand themselves and their situation more fully, so that they can make better decisions in the future.

Notice that we have not said 'make the *right* decision.' If from a Lead or Manage perspective there is only one decision that can be made, then the nature of the conversation changes. In this case you would want to clearly communicate the decision that the team member should have made and coach them to enable them to understand how to make better decisions in the future.

In time-pressured environments, and through misunderstanding the skills of people management, many of us are inclined to believe the way we would do something is the *right* way of doing it. Ian tells a story about how one of his first managers had a tendency to give very specific, step-by-step instructions on how to get to a desired outcome. The challenge was that Ian often felt he could see a quicker and more efficient way to achieve the same result. Fortunately, Ian's manager was often required to be out of the office and, having given his instructions, would leave. As long as the result was achieved before he returned, the manager never asked how it had been done. It often turned out that there was more than one way to deliver the required outcome.

Many of us think in black and white – right and wrong – thinking that our way is the only way. Life is rarely this simple and people who are managed from this perspective quickly become disengaged team members – even if they remain compliant. To become great team leaders, we need to embrace the expertise in our teams and develop a finely honed ability to identify when to use Lead, when to use Manage and when to use Coach.

Just as we said in *Chapter 7* regarding the reality phase of the GROW model, the primary function of Coach mode is to understand – not to solve, fix, heal, make better or be wise, but to understand. The magic is that it is in that moment of understanding that the team member understands for themself, becomes more aware, and is then in a position to make better decisions and choices than they would have made previously.

In this way, coaching is profoundly simple and simply profound. But most of us struggle to get above our own agenda and instead want to be seen to be making a difference.

One way of managing our own ego is to allow a conversation to follow the interest of the person we are talking with (see *Chapter 6*). As you do, the team member with whom you are talking will gain clarity and understanding that will enable them to make better decisions going forward.

Listening to understand

Next time you are in a position where someone else is speaking, take the opportunity to notice your own listening. If you are like the rest of us, the quality of it will be inconsistent, and probably dependent on your level of interest in what is being said. In some moments your attention will be completely with the speaker; in others it will drift. A particular point may hold your attention and you begin to relate it to some other matter … and all of a sudden you are away with the fairies. Perhaps the speaker is a little boring, or maybe they don't express themselves well. Your own judgements creep in, followed, in short order, by your expectations, opinions and assumptions. Even as you read this page, your thoughts might spin off in some flight of fantasy, or something in the environment may distract you.

Listening is a fundamental skill and one might think that paying attention should be easy. But most of us are not that good at it.

Sometimes, in a workshop, we will give the participants a simple listening exercise. When the exercise is over, we ask them what got in the way of their listening – what were the interferences? – and will note down their responses.

Here is a typical list:

- "Other people talking."
- "What I thought they were going to say."
- "What I thought they should say."
- "They were boring."
- "I had already worked out what they should do."
- "I had thought of what they were saying already."
- "What I was thinking was more interesting."
- "I was thinking of the next question."
- "I was thinking of my response."
- "What's for dinner?"
- "Why is he wearing that tie?"

That little voice in your head works overtime, and it is difficult to stop it. There is so much going on in our own minds that making sufficient space for another person is difficult. At this point in the workshop, some participants get upset. Perhaps because they value their own thoughts and ideas, are entertained by their assumptions and revel in their judgements. This is fine, of course, as long as they do not try to coach someone or pretend that they are listening.

Many of us listen not with the intention to understand but with the intention to respond. We are just waiting for the speaker to take a breath so that we can get to speak or – almost as bad – using the time when the other is speaking to think up the next question or a suitable response. Some years ago, when Myles did some work with an international consultancy where the consultants were renowned for their intelligence, a senior partner informed him, "People around here don't listen, they reload!"

Imagine a spring-loaded stack of plates such as you might find in a canteen. As you take the top plate, the next one is pushed up. Each plate represents an idea or notion that rises into your consciousness. As a thought enters the consciousness and is passed on to a listener, the space for the next thought is created. And that one is passed on, followed by the next one. Somewhere down in your stack of plates – in your mind – is a solution, a creative idea, an insight. If someone is willing to listen, you may get to that plate – that thought. And because the thought is uniquely your own, you will nurture it, develop it and put it to some creative use.

On the other hand, if your team leader takes the first few plates, assumes that they now understand, and then gives them back to you, adding a few more plates of their own – their own good ideas, or their way forward – then no real learning will occur and you do not own the outcome. Not only does this mean the solution, idea or insight is now further down the stack, it also means that in order to get to it, you have to challenge your team leader's authority. Another good idea lost, another breakthrough unheard – and you are left demotivated. And as it is for you, so it will be for members of your team.

Try noticing when you are *not* listening, and gently bring your attention back to the speaker. This has one tiny flaw as a tactic, in that the only time you become aware that you have 'gone away with your thoughts' is when you return or when the speaker gives you some feedback – which may be too late. If this does happen, the only response that has any integrity is to own up. The speaker is unlikely to be surprised; they will have noticed, probably before you did.

A GAME TO PLAY

1. Think of a personal quality you would like to bring to your role (e.g. direction, empathy or urgency).
2. At the beginning of the day, give yourself a score between 1 and 10 (where 1 is very weak and 10 is very strong) according to how present you feel this quality is in you.
3. Score yourself at lunchtime.
4. Score yourself again at the end of the day.
5. How did the scores change?
6. What did you notice about the way you showed up to work?

WANT TO KNOW MORE?

How to Listen: Tools for Opening Up Conversations When It Matters Most by Katie Colombus[41]

The skills of listening are essential for those who manage others in the workplace. Where better to turn for a description of those skills than The Samaritans? The skills used in supporting others to face life's challenges are ultimately the same skills required by the Enabling Manager.

CHAPTER 9

Developing Your Skills as an Enabling Manager, Part 1: Asking Great Questions

With the three core skills covered in *Chapters 6, 7* and *8* in mind (following interest, raising awareness and listening to understand), we can now turn our attention to the two further skill sets that are critical to coaching: how to ask great questions and how to go about proposing your own thoughts without disempowering your team.

When we are teaching coaching skills, we are often asked for a list of 'great questions.' These lists exist and you can even buy books that will give you a set of questions to use when you are coaching. You may find such lists helpful but our experience suggests that if you give the person you are listening to your full attention, with the intent of generating understanding and clarity, then you will ask great questions. If, while the other person is talking, you are trying to remember that great question you read somewhere, then you will not be giving them your full attention and, even if you remember it, your 'great' question will not be as helpful as you imagine.

The questions that appear throughout the remainder of this chapter may seem obvious but it is the *intent* behind your choice of question that makes them effective. At this point it may be helpful to revisit the GROW model (see *Chapter 7)* and think in terms of the intent of the questions at each stage of the model:

- **T (Topic)**: to listen to understand the broad topic
- **G (Goal):** to establish the desired outcome of the conversation
- **R (Reality):** to listen to get the clearest understanding of the topic possible
- **(Options):** to generate a range of options to move the topic forward
- **W (Wrap-up):** to agree the next steps

Questions that clarify

When it comes to creating clarity, there are just five words you need to remember – and they are familiar to us all:

- What
- Who
- Where
- When
- How

Notice that we have not included *why*. We'll come back to that one shortly.

WHAT

What – or, better still, 'what specifically is that?' – is useful when someone uses a word that you have not come across before.

> **Team member:** And so, without telling anyone, they removed all the codals.
> **Team leader:** What specifically is a codal?
> (*We cannot take this example any further because in order to make the point, we had to find a noun that no one would know. So, we made one up.*)

In most meetings, it would not be the end of the world if you did not understand a particular word. You would merely wait for the break and ask a trusted colleague. In a conversation driven by the need to understand, you simply cannot afford to miss the meaning. *What* is also useful when a team member uses a word that you do recognize but that could mean any number of things.

> **Team member:** In this company I get absolutely no acknowledgement.
> **Team leader:** What do you mean by acknowledgement?
> **Team member:** A little bit of praise now and again.

You see, the team leader assumption might have been that the salary was acknowledgement enough!

WHO

Who is useful in two ways. The first way is when someone uses a pronoun (e.g. 'he,' 'she,' 'they' or 'it') but you are not sure who is being referred to.

Team member: I think most people are saying that they are unhappy with the new system.
Team leader: Let me just check that. Who specifically said that?

The second way is to get a complete list of all the people that might have an impact on the topic of the conversation. For example, 'Who else is involved? Who are the other members of the team?'

WHERE AND WHEN

Where and *when* give specific locations in time and place. In the following example, a worry is identified as something very specific, and you can coach the team member to enable them to draw out the conclusions of the report.

Team member: I am completely stuck with this report.
Team leader: Where exactly in the report are you stuck?
Team member: Well, the main part of it is fine, I'm just having difficulty drawing out the conclusions for the summary.

In the next example, a loose commitment that could easily be misunderstood – "soon" could mean a few minutes or a few weeks – quickly becomes a firm agreement.

Team member: I'll talk to Paul soon.
Team leader: When exactly?
Team member: Tomorrow, before 12.

HOW

How is a useful question. It is always used in connection with verbs – 'doing' words. It gets to high-quality information very quickly.

Team member: I need to get Eric and Frida fully engaged in the launch.
Team leader: Right. How might you engage them?
Team member: First, I can explain why it's so important to the business. And then I can ask which parts of it are most interesting to each of them.

How much usually adds clarity and raises awareness when matters of quantity, size or scale are under discussion.

There is another version of the *how much* question that has a very similar intent: to raise awareness.

Team member: I am really concerned about the new strategy Bob presented yesterday.
Team leader: How concerned, on a scale of one to ten?
Team member: That's a good question. Actually, only about three or four.
Team leader: So, do we need to discuss it now?
Team member: No, it's more important that we talk through the conference next week.

If the response to the *how much* question had been eight, then there would have been no doubt that the team member and team leader would have needed to talk about Bob's new strategy.

WHY NOT TO USE *WHY*

We have excluded *why* from our list of questions that clarify. More often than not, *why* elicits reasons, justifications and excuses – none of which are useful in raising awareness. 'Why?' is also a pretty sloppy question. It can mean so many things, from 'What is your purpose?' to 'What is your reason?' to the blame-filled 'But why?'

Instead, you should ask a more specific question:

- "What is your purpose in that?"
- "What were the reasons behind that decision?"
- "What is it that makes that important for you?"

Some other questions

Other types of question have no obvious category but can be very effective. One common pitfall of team leaders is to assume that there is an agreed way forward when in fact there is not. Tying people down to specifics and getting them to commit are important parts of your toolkit. These are aspects of the skill of challenging, which we address in the next chapter.

GET SPECIFIC

Team member: Well, that has been a useful conversation. I'll try a couple of the things we discussed over the next few weeks.

Team leader: Great. Tell me, what specifically are you going to do? And by when?

COMMIT

Team member: I think I might have a go at giving Paul some feedback.

Team leader: You sound a little unsure. What are you actually going to do?

ASKING GREAT QUESTIONS: A SUMMARY

If you are completely focused and also interested in your team member's learning, your natural instinct to coach will manifest and you will ask an appropriate question. In any case, it usually doesn't matter if you make a mistake. Conversations are not exams, and you do not get only one chance. If a question doesn't work, ask another. When you are in a good relationship, it does not matter.

A THOUGHT EXPERIMENT TO TRY

Think of an issue that is challenging you at the moment. Write yourself a short summary.

Use *what*, *who*, *where*, *when* and *how* questions to interrogate the issue.

What will you do differently going forward?

WANT TO KNOW MORE?

The Coaching Manual: The Definitive Guide to the Process, Principles and Skills of Personal Coaching by Julie Starr[42]
Another recommended read for those wanting to dig deeper into the skills of coaching.

CHAPTER 10

Developing Your Skills as an Enabling Manager, Part 2: Proposing

Effective team leaders know how to provide direction and instruction without disempowering their team. Using these skills well enables you to fulfil your responsibility of keeping your team on track without resorting to a command-and-control approach.

Returning to the jigsaw analogy in *Chapter 7*, there will be times when you are coaching a team member, helping them to think for themselves, and it becomes clear that they are missing a piece of the puzzle. You may choose to keep coaching to see whether they can find it themselves. Or, on other occasions, it may become clear that they will not find the missing piece themselves. How can you help them find the piece?

Let's explore this a bit more. Sometimes as a team leader you will find yourself listening to a team member as they think out loud and you will find a thought occurs to you that might add value to their thinking. The trouble is that sharing your thought may distract the team member, or it may take responsibility for a decision away from them.

Let's assume that you want to leave responsibility with the team member but you want to throw your thoughts into the mix. How do you go about sharing your thoughts without taking over the thinking process?

Proposing requires a different skill set from raising awareness or generating understanding (see *Chapter 8*) as it covers the skills you need when you choose to make an input rather than drawing information from your team member. One part of the definition of 'propose,' given in *The Chambers Dictionary 11th edition* 2008 is 'to put forward or exhibit, to bring to one's own or another person's attention.' 'To bring to another person's attention' is particularly appropriate, as it acknowledges that while you may, for example, make a suggestion, the team member does not have to include it in their thinking or act on it. To propose is not to impose.

Your intent in proposing should be to make your observations, knowledge, experience, intelligence, insight, intuition and wisdom available to the team member to enable them to understand themselves and their situation more fully, so that they can make better decisions than they would have done otherwise.

The following are the specific skills of proposing:

- Giving feedback
- Making suggestions
- Giving advice
- Instructing
- Challenging
- Evoking creativity
- Ensuring transparency

The remainder of this chapter considers each skill in turn.

Giving feedback

Unfortunately, giving and receiving feedback are both optional – it could not be any other way. But you have only to ask two questions of people in most organizations to be very clear that there is not a whole lot of it happening.

The first question is this: "Have you given any feedback recently?" The answer is almost always "Yes." Then you ask: "Have you received any feedback recently?" The answer is invariably "No." One of two possibilities must be the case: either, somewhere in the organization, one person is getting all the feedback and is therefore incredibly clear on their strengths and weaknesses – or not much feedback is being given.

A third and more generous conclusion is that people think they are giving feedback when in fact they are merely alluding to something or dropping hints. Whichever is the case, the vast majority of us do not receive sufficient feedback.

This is an important issue. We need feedback to function properly. The consequence of not receiving feedback is that we make it up ourselves. Some years ago, while working with a client, we discovered that the members of a small team were feeling very deflated. All of them were considering leaving because they were sure they were about to be made redundant. The company had recently moved every other team into another building, leaving just 10 people in a building that could house over 30. We knew that the directors were creating space in anticipation of a rapid increase in staffing but they had not communicated their plan and were in danger of losing valuable members of their team. In the absence of communication, people make stuff up.

In workshops, it can be useful to ask people what stops them from giving feedback. A typical list of responses includes these ideas:

- "It's not part of my job."
- "If they can't do the job, they should not be here."
- "It's not in the culture."
- "I don't have time."
- "I don't have enough information."
- "Who am I to judge another?"
- "I don't want to discourage them."
- "I don't want to hurt them."

When pushed, most people will acknowledge that not giving feedback comes down to that last answer: "I don't want to hurt them." Underneath is another, unspoken response that we think it's worth being really clear about, and it is this: "If I hurt you, you will not like me any more." It's an understandable – but hardly noble – reason for withholding feedback.

Before we go any further, we want to put something to bed. There is no such thing as negative feedback and there is no such thing as positive feedback. There is just feedback – data. What happens is that people attach a judgement to the data to suit their purpose in that moment. That purpose is usually 'to be right.' And then the receiver responds to the judgement and not to the data. 'The boss is angry, so I won't do that again' is not a great way of getting to a good decision. As a team leader, your role is to give the data as cleanly as possible, so that a team member can receive it, assess it and make their own decision about how to proceed.

That said, in giving feedback, it is nigh on impossible to communicate only the data. The receiver will also get some sense of your intent and the emotional charge that you carry. We must distinguish carefully between these three aspects of feedback:

- **Data:** This needs to be of the highest quality you can identify – the more specific, the better. It also needs to be something that you have observed. Second-hand information frustrates people, because they cannot effectively challenge it. Examples help. Keep it free from judgement and interpretation.
- **Intent:** You must be really clear about your intent in giving the feedback. If it is to prove yourself right or to get one up on the receiver, it will not work. The only intent that has integrity is to raise awareness.
- **Emotional charge:** Are you angry, disappointed or elated? Whatever your emotions are, they will be communicated to some degree. You simply cannot help it. It is often useful to acknowledge this explicitly, so that you can manage yourself better.

GIVING FEEDBACK IN EVERYDAY WORK LIFE

There is a useful three-step process to remember for giving feedback in the course of everyday work life:

- Contract
- Data
- Action

The contract is the agreement you make with the person to whom you wish to give feedback. Ideally, the contract includes an offer and clarity of intent. It might look like this:

Team leader (TL): I have some feedback for you. Do you want it?

Usually, the answer is "Yes." If it is "No," it might be appropriate to check the reason behind the rejection of the offer.

> **TL:** I appreciate that you don't want my feedback. May I ask why?
>
> **Team member (TM):** I'm really busy right now. Could we speak later?

Or:

> **TM:** This is not a good place – it's too public. Can we use your office?

If the offer of feedback has been turned down and it is a critical management issue, you might have to insist on giving the feedback.

> **TL:** I appreciate that you are not interested in my feedback, but it is my view that your approach to these meetings is jeopardizing the whole project. So, I have a responsibility to give you the feedback. Do you want to have it now or later?

The second element of the contract, clarity of intent, is demonstrated in the previous example, in which the team leader explains why it is so important for them to provide the feedback. Another example is this: "I want to make sure you are successful in running these meetings."

As mentioned above, your data (the second step) should be of the highest quality possible, observed and owned by you, without judgement or interpretation. If it is a weighty matter, you might ask the team member to self-assess: "How do you see it?"

You should usually ensure that your data covers three key areas: situation, behaviour and impact.

TL: In this afternoon's meeting about the Odyssey Project, when you questioned Jack (*situation*) I thought you were a little abrupt with him (*behaviour*). He seemed to me to be upset and demotivated as a result (*impact*).

Finally, your feedback will almost certainly be ineffectual if there is no clarity or agreement about the action the team member will take next. If it is a complex issue, they may require further coaching, though you should not assume that you will be the coach. A simple question will often be sufficient: "How might you help Jack get motivated again?" More generic examples include: "How could you approach this kind of situation in the future?" and "How, specifically, will you take this forward from here?"

GIVING FEEDBACK WHEN YOU ARE COACHING

Many of the guidelines suggested above hold true for giving feedback when you are coaching. It is still important that you don't make an assumption that the team member will welcome the feedback. If you have chosen to be non-directive (see *Chapter 6*) but then, suddenly and uninvited, you come out with some feedback, it can be disruptive and can upset your relationship with the team member. The key is to offer the feedback, clearly signalling that this is a change of style. Then, once the feedback has been delivered, you should return to following interest.

Team leader (TL): I've got some feedback for you. Do you want it?

Team member (TM): Yes, I'd welcome your view.

TL: What I have noticed is … (*provides details in directive style, then returns to following interest style*) How does that fit in with what you've been saying? Is that worth considering?

Occasionally, someone will say "No" when you offer to give feedback. When this happens in a coaching situation, it is almost always because they are busy thinking through another part of the issue and don't want to interrupt that process. When they are ready, you can give the feedback. If they still don't want it – which would be quite strange – don't give it. If a pattern emerges in terms of a team member continually refusing feedback, you might instead give feedback on the repeated refusals.

Making suggestions

Suggestions are ideas that you believe to be appropriate to the situation under discussion. They arise in your mind as a function of your experience, intelligence, intuition or imagination. They are occasionally valid and will sometimes be acceptable to a team member. As with feedback, the key issue is whether you can present them to the team member in such a way as to give them a genuine choice about whether to accept them or not.

The issue of choice can be influenced by a number of factors: your power in the relationship, your ability to influence, the team member's desire to be influenced or the team member's wish not to have to take responsibility. There is a complexity here that no number of written words could completely resolve, so let us return to what you *can* do. The guidelines are not dissimilar to those for offering feedback:

- Always present your suggestions as an offer: "I've got a suggestion. Would you like to hear it?"
- When the suggestion has been heard, return to following interest: "Does that work for you?" or "We've identified a number of suggestions – *w*, *x*, *y* and the one I threw in, *z*. Which of those is the most interesting?"

Giving advice

There are obviously times when, as a team leader, you will need to give advice but when you have chosen to coach, you should think twice about doing this. Offering advice suggests that you are not seeing the situation from the same place as the team member with whom you are talking. When you give advice, you are implying that you have knowledge and experience that lead to a view that your team member could not have reached for themselves.

We are, of course, presenting a rather narrow interpretation of advice. If you find yourself in the position of giving advice, the guidelines are the same as for any time you move away from following interest. Make an offer and, if the advice is wanted, give it. Once it has been heard, return to following interest so that the team member is left with a choice about whether to accept the advice.

Giving permission to the other person to experiment with the advice you've given can enable them to make the advice their own. For example: "Now you've heard that advice, how might you use it going forward?"

Instructing

Giving instructions implies that there is a technique or approach that you know but that the team member could not work out for themselves, or that it would take more time than is available for them to work out for themselves. We can often tell ourselves that we know more than the people in our team, but often our knowledge just gets in the way of team members' learning. These are some of the times, however, when instructing might be appropriate:

- When the team member is tired
- When there is significant time pressure
- When the team member is upset or panicking
- When the technique is complex (and known to you)

The reality, of course, is that you can tell anyone to do anything – they just might not do it. Some people will do what you say, but that will be either because they have surrendered their authority to you or because they are unwilling to challenge your right to instruct. In either case, their compliance is likely to lack enthusiasm and commitment.

Challenging

We have put this skill in this chapter on proposing, although it could just as well sit in the chapter on raising awareness and generating understanding (*Chapter 8*). Although challenging arises from the team leader's understanding, its function is to raise awareness. True challenge comes from a belief in potential.

Myles remembers coaching Mike, a senior manager in a large UK-based retail organization. Mike had been given a project to restructure a major division of the organization, which would lead to some redundancies, but there were no clear objectives behind the project. When asked how he could identify some, Mike said that he could talk to his boss, who had given him the task. Myles asked him when he might do this. Mike virtually collapsed in his chair and looked as if the air had been sucked out of him.

> "I don't know that I want to go through all the trouble," he said.
> "Why not?" Myles replied.
> "I am thinking of leaving the business."
> "You're thinking of this – or you've decided?"
> "I am not sure."

At this point Myles became really clear. Here was a highly intelligent and caring man who had given up. This was not a person acting to his potential. Myles challenged him, as he was unwilling to see Mike renounce his authority.

> "Listen, if you don't get clear objectives from your boss, you immediately eliminate one option from your choices – because if you're not successful in this project, you could lose your job. Tell me, how are you going to get clear objectives for the restructuring?"

Mike sat up and talked through his options. When this part of the conversation was complete, Myles asked him how he would go about deciding whether to stay in the organization or not. Further action steps emerged. Mike left the meeting walking on air. Sure, nothing had been resolved, but he was now in control of what he could do to change the situation.

In challenging, it is particularly important to check your intent. 'Being right' in the moment helps no one. As we have said, a true challenge comes from a belief in another's potential.

Evoking creativity

Enabling creativity is a vital part of your work as a team leader. It is what allows the people in your team to break out of a difficult situation, invent a new future or possibility, and make a step change in their productivity or quality of life. It shows up in many ways, but the two that we will focus on here are concerned with creating the future ('visioning' and 'goal-setting') and innovation (new ways of doing things, new options).

It is very easy to fall into accepting what is apparently reasonable, in the sense of what could reasonably be achieved. For instance, when someone is creating a vision for their career, we may have an idea of what is possible for that person, or what they are capable of achieving. When that set of judgements shows up in the conversation, it has the potential to limit it.

The same thing can happen in the options stage of the GROW model (see *Chapter 7*). A team member comes up with a list of options within the confines of what is reasonable, and you go along with it. Now, we are not adherents of the school of thought that says you can have whatever you dream of. There are some things that limit us – at least in this stage of our evolution. But we are absolutely certain that there is much, much more available to us than we might think, if only we dare look.

Evoking creativity, then, is about how we can respectfully challenge members of our team, and perhaps ourselves, to look beyond what is merely reasonable and scale the heights of the extraordinary.

TECHNIQUES FOR CREATING THE FUTURE

The simplest technique for creating the future is to create a vision. Agree a time frame that makes sense to the team member (such as the end of the year, one year or five years). Ask them to think of all the things that might be possible within that time frame. Ask them to suggest as many ideas as they can. When they have done that, ask them to edit the list down to the things they are willing to commit to.

If you want to get creative, you might also consider getting them to write a speech – that would be given at a certain date in the future – recounting their successes and accomplishments.

TECHNIQUES FOR EVOKING INNOVATION

Sometimes you will need to encourage team members to move beyond what they think is possible and create some more innovative options.

To start with simply ask the team member to create a list of all the possible options, keep asking "And what else?" until there are no more ideas. Then, to unlock more creative ideas, you might try asking, "If you had a magic wand, what would you do?" or "What is the most outrageous option you can think of?" These questions work by removing limitations and can free up thinking.

Ensuring transparency and using the four tests

In completing this chapter on the skills of proposing, it is important to remember the intent behind this skill set: to make available your observations, knowledge, experience, intelligence, insight, intuition and wisdom. The skills of proposing are the most difficult to deploy because of the inherent danger of removing responsibility and choice from the members of your team.

Here are two techniques that are helpful in avoiding this danger. One is the idea of transparency (which we will return to in *Chapter 11* in the context of building a good working relationship with your team) and the other we call the 'four tests.'

TRANSPARENCY

Being transparent means that your intentions for your team are completely clear to the team members. Two examples you might use are: "My intention in giving you this feedback is to help you understand the impact of your behaviour" and "This is a marathon and not a sprint, and I am concerned about the size of your workload."

There is a slightly different use of transparency that also helps when you are proposing. What we suggest is that you signal clearly to the team member what mode you are in – Lead, Manage or Coach. This lets them know that you are aware of when you are being directive and when you are enabling them to think for themselves.

For example: "Putting my lead hat on for a moment, we probably need to keep in mind what we've been tasked to achieve." Having reminded them of the context of their work, you can then immediately return to following interest: "Of the options you came up with, which ones align with our brief?"

THE FOUR TESTS

The four tests operate in a different way. You can use them when you notice that you have something to propose, such as a suggestion to offer or some feedback to give. If you are not sure that it is the right thing to do, you can ask yourself the following four questions:

- Will it raise awareness?
- Will it leave responsibility and choice with the other person?
- Is the relationship strong enough to withstand the intervention (i.e. is there sufficient trust in my intention)?
- What is my intent?

If the answer to the first three questions is "Yes" and your intent is congruent with the suggested intent behind this skill set, you can go ahead.

Postscript

To finish this chapter, we offer a cautionary tale. Many years ago, Myles was coaching a senior employee, Jim, in a large management consultancy. After the third meeting, Myles asked for some feedback. In responding, Jim made a request.

"I would like more from you," he said.
"More what?" Myles asked.
"More input – more suggestions and feedback."

Myles complied with the request at the next session, and by the end of the meeting he was feeling quite dissatisfied. He could see Jim was too, but on the day Myles did not have the necessary courage to ask for more feedback.

It so happened that the following day Myles had to give a demonstration of tennis coaching to a very discerning audience. He knew that if he made the slightest suggestion, rather than following interest, it would be picked up, so he was determined to be as 'clean' as possible. It was a great session, and it reminded Myles of what constituted effective coaching. It also caused him to reflect on his coaching of Jim.

Taking a more directive stance had clearly not helped and, as Myles thought about it, he realized that in the earlier meetings he had been too polite with his questioning and had not helped Jim really clarify his thinking. In the next meeting, Myles listened even more intently and made sure that he really understood everything Jim was saying. Myles applied the GROW model with more precision, making sure to establish a clear outcome from the conversation.

The conversation finished in less than an hour – about half the normal time. Jim had worked so hard that he was almost perspiring. As Myles left the meeting room, Jim turned and said, "That was hard work. You really made me think. Thank you."

A THOUGHT EXPERIMENT TO TRY

Think of a situation where you feel you will need to give someone feedback. Before going to speak with them, work through these four tests:

- Will it raise awareness?
- Will it leave responsibility and choice with the other person?
- Is the relationship strong enough to withstand the intervention (i.e. is there sufficient trust in your intention)?
- What is your intent?

If you still think it appropriate to give feedback, use the three-step process outlined in this chapter (contract, data, action) to think through what you want to say.

WANT TO KNOW MORE?

Creative Confidence: Unleashing the Creative Potential Within Us All by Tom Kelley and David Kelley[43]
A book full of ideas about how to inspire and maintain creative confidence in your team.

Group Genius: The Creative Power of Collaboration by Keith Sawyer[44]
This is a fascinating book that explores the creativity of jazz groups, theatre ensembles and conversation analysis. Discover how to encourage group creativity and unlock the genius of a team.

CHAPTER 11

Relate: Building and Maintaining a Solid Foundation

Every business and organization is essentially a coming together of people to achieve specific outcomes. Developing and maintaining good relationships with your team is the foundation of effective team leadership.

The Enabling Leader model has an important foundation stone, and the skills of Lead – Manage – Coach stand or fall on the integrity of this foundation. To succeed as a team leader, it is vital that you build and nurture the relationship you have with each member of your team.

On our travels, we meet people who have reached senior positions without understanding this dynamic. They tend to be very task-focused leaders who see the idea of workplace relationships as 'fluffy' and 'a waste of time.' It doesn't take much digging to see that, despite their numerous promotions, their team is nowhere near as effective as it could be.

You can climb the ladder of business without paying attention to your relationships with your team but, at some point, the ladder will prove too fragile to continue to support you.

It is clear that people flourish and produce their best work when they feel recognized and valued as people. This being the case, you can see how important it is to get to know your team – to build trust and to communicate your appreciation for them as people, not just for their work.

Building trust-based relationships

What comes first, trust or trustworthiness? Ask that question in a group of people and you will find you have an interesting conversation on your hands. Some will jump in straight away to argue that trust comes first. Then, the more risk averse will point out that to trust a team member is to put your reputation in their hands, asking "Why would you do that without evidence that they are trustworthy?"

The conversation will usually resolve into the idea that the process starts with the team leader trusting someone in small ways and builds to a fully trusting relationship. Then comes the question of how long that takes and a whole other can of worms is opened up. The reality is that, if you want your team to be the best it can be, you don't have lots of time to build trust.

Why build trust-based relationships?

Trust-based relationships enable people to work together effectively and efficiently to produce higher-quality outcomes. When team leaders don't trust their teams, they fall into micromanaging – constantly checking that people are doing the right thing, in the right way, at the right time. This reduces the effectiveness of both the team leader – who is spending too much time focused on other people's work – and the team members – who become annoyed as they feel undermined.

One interesting dynamic of changing work practices came to the fore during the Covid-19 pandemic. With a large part of the workforce working from home, a question arose in the minds of some managers – "How do I know that they are putting in the hours?" The result was a huge uptake in the use of monitoring technology.[45] Businesses put in place monitoring software that could tell what programs were running on employees' laptops, how much time was spent on different tasks and whether or not individual employees were at their desk as much as they were meant to be. The most extreme versions of this software gave managers the ability to use the webcam on employees' laptops to see whether they were at their desk. Unsurprisingly, this software kills productivity and turns even the best employees into clock-watchers.

The pandemic accelerated changing work trends and many office-based jobs will never return to the office-based, five-day-a-week, nine-to-five job. The chances are that your team is rarely all in the same place at the same time. You may sometimes wonder how members of your team use their time when they are working from home. Trust has become even more important than it was.

Trust is the foundation of effective communication. It removes barriers, such as preconceived ideas, limiting beliefs and doubts about each other's intent. It also fosters a sense of belonging, commitment to 'the cause' and enjoyment of work. All of this enables high-quality work to be delivered effectively and efficiently. When you need your team to be open, share ideas and collaborate, trust is essential.

So, what does a trust-based relationship look like? Here are six characteristics:

- Belief in each other's positive intentions
- Respect for each other
- Open and honest communications
- Feedback and challenge
- Acceptance and understanding
- Holding each other accountable

These in turn deliver any number of benefits, including:

- Better business outcomes
- Better problem-solving, analysis and creativity
- Quicker responses
- More effective teamwork
- More enjoyment

How to build trust-based relationships

There are four practices that, when combined, will enable you to build and sustain trust-based relationships:

- Recognize that working together you can achieve more than you could on your own
- Be willing to disclose relevant information and respond without hesitation (i.e. be transparent)
- Connect emotionally and commit to the relationship for the long run
- Understand others' perspectives and adapt accordingly

To get the best out of your team, it is important that you pay attention to all four practices, and the skills of Lead – Manage – Coach will enable you to do that.

It is worth taking the time to think about each of these practices in turn.

WORK TOGETHER

It may sound obvious, but a trust-based relationship requires you to agree on the facts and the reality of the situation. We all have our own interpretation of reality, and it is important to take time to ensure that everyone has the same view. Be aware that sometimes two people can use the same words to describe different things. As a team leader, you must develop the skill of exploring what people mean by the words they use.

Once you have agreement on the facts and the reality of a situation, you can look at moving forward together. Ensure that your team is aligned on shared goals, how decisions will be made and the way forward.

DO

- Share goals and plans
- Offer and ask for support
- Make joint commitments
- Be willing to compromise

DON'T

- Put your own needs first
- Focus only on your own goals
- Make promises you can't keep
- Try to 'win' disagreements

BE TRANSPARENT

When you develop personal transparency, you will find others in your team will respond in kind. Being transparent about your intentions and motivations builds trust. Of course, to do this you need to spend time noticing and developing an awareness of your own beliefs, goals and emotions.

DO

- Share information and insights
- Examine your own goals, beliefs and emotions
- Communicate your intent
- Be honest

DON'T

- Withhold feedback and perspectives
- Expect people to know or guess at your intent

MAKE EMOTIONAL CONNECTIONS

When people feel understood and valued, they create emotional connections with the people around them and feel comfortable in the team. Take time to build connections with people in your team and commit to your relationship with them.

DO

- Share what's important to you
- Look for connections
- Listen for what's important

DON'T

- Ignore requests and offers of support
- Dwell or focus on differences and disagreements

TAKE TIME TO SEE THROUGH THE EYES OF OTHERS

Seeing things from someone else's perspective is an important skill. When you can understand the needs and perspectives of your team, you can adapt your actions and behaviours appropriately. Of course, the best way to see through the eyes of others is to avoid assumptions and ask questions with the intent of understanding their perspective.

DO

- See things from the other person's perspective
- Understand what is important to the other person
- Adapt your actions to match the other person's needs

DON'T

- Act as if your viewpoint is the truth
- Avoid emotions
- Brush aside upsets

A THOUGHT EXPERIMENT TO TRY

What don't you currently share with your team?

For each thing you identify, ask yourself the following questions:

- What would happen if you were more open about this?
- What would not happen if you were more open about this?
- What would happen if you didn't share this?
- What would not happen if you didn't share this?

WANT TO KNOW MORE?

Dare to Lead: Brave Work, Tough Conversations, Whole Hearts by Brené Brown[46]
Brené Brown promotes a view of leadership that is based on empathy, connection and courage. This is an important book for those wanting to understand the kind of leadership needed today.

Lead. Care. Win. How to Become a Leader Who Matters by Dan Pontefract[47]
Dan Pontefract makes the case for leadership based on meaningful, respectful relationships.

CHAPTER 12

Using Lead – Manage – Coach in Your Day-to-Day Role

So far, we have covered the underlying principles, the key models and many of the skills of the enabling manager, and we have tried to give a sense of what this role looks like in practice. In this chapter, we want to show you how the idea fits within the context of your organization, and specifically your role as a team leader. Crucially, we want to look at how using Lead – Manage – Coach as an approach can benefit both the business *and* the people in your team.

In our workshops, we sometimes ask the participants – all managers – what the *purpose* of management is. Specifically: "When whoever it was invented the notion of management, what was the problem they were trying to solve?"

The answers we get are generally not very good. In fact, in one workshop, as we discussed the topic further and introduced the idea of enabling a team to be the best they can be, one guy looked up and said, "But this is not how I think of my job." And therein lies the problem. Most managers think of their job in terms of their trade, discipline or profession. The title 'manager' is thought of in terms of status and increased remuneration; it is not really thought of as an entirely new set of responsibilities.

Few managers get out of bed in the morning and think, "What can I do today to help my team be brilliant?" That's just not what the job is as they see it. So, the argument that follows concerns the nature of management, and it starts with some observations about a fundamental dynamic in any company: the relationship between the individual employee and the organization itself.

The individual and the organization

Individuals join organizations so that they can achieve some of their goals. These goals can be simple – to make enough money to pay the mortgage – or they may be complex – to satisfy a need to make a meaningful contribution. Equally, these goals can be well thought out and clear or reactive and ambiguous.

An organization employs individuals to fulfil its mission and achieve its goals. Typically, the goals are, if not clear, at least explicit, so those responsible seek employees who have the right skills to fit in with those goals as well as compatible values.

A successful relationship between an individual and an organization is achieved when both parties achieve their own goals (see *Figure 7*). This is a fundamental dynamic in any organization; if it is entirely neglected, people leave, and ultimately what that means is that there is no organization.

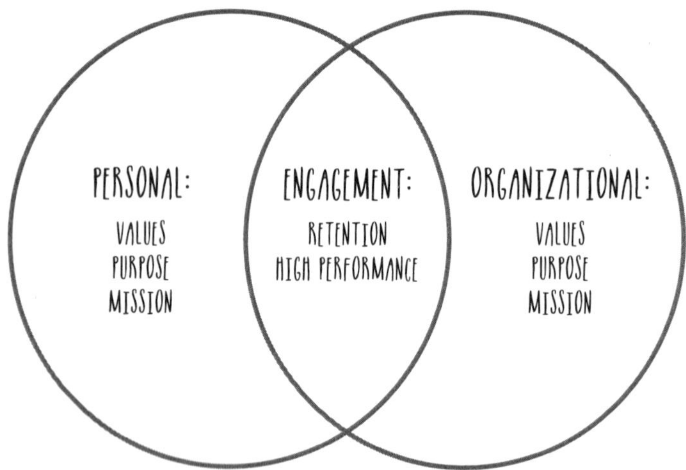

FIGURE 7 **THE INTERSECTION BETWEEN INDIVIDUAL AND ORGANIZATIONAL GOALS**

The individual obviously has a significant responsibility in ensuring the success of the relationship, as does the organization. The organization will give authority to a number of people to ensure that its responsibilities are met. Some of this is laid at the door of HR professionals, but by far the greatest share of an organization's responsibility rests with managers and team leaders. It is their job to ensure that both parties' needs are satisfied.

This brings us back to the model at the heart of this book, shown in *Figure 8*.

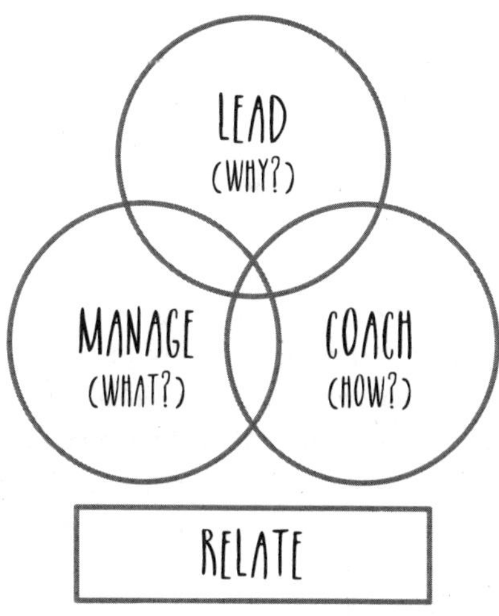

FIGURE 8 **THE ENABLING LEADER MODEL**

Back in *Chapter 3*, we defined the four elements of the model. These might be summarized as follows:

- **Lead:** ensure the team member understands *why* what they are doing is important
- **Manage:** ensure the team member has complete clarity about *what* they need to do and agrees to do it
- **Coach:** ensure the team member has clarity about *how* they will approach and execute their role and achieve their goals
- **Relate:** for a real conversation to happen, there needs to be trust

Organizational and individual authority

To really understand how the Enabling Leader model applies in practice, there is an underlying issue that must be considered. This is the issue of authority. Typically, authority refers to the power to decree something, by right or office, and to get it done by oneself or others.

In order to be an effective team leader, it is imperative to understand the nature of authority and where it lies. Back in *Chapter 1*, we briefly reviewed how the way in which people respond to authority has changed. People's desire for autonomy is, in the end, a desire for authority over their own choices and actions.

There is an appropriate balance to be struck between individual or personal and organizational authority, and the team leader, caught in the middle, needs to understand how to strike it. Sometimes, individuals get together with other individuals and agree to share authority so that they can achieve something together that they cannot achieve apart – like a marriage. And, to make this successful, the individual parties have to surrender some of their authority to the whole. Similarly, organizations and individuals can get together. Employment is a relationship.

Individuals have authority. By this, we mean that there are areas of their lives where they can make decisions and execute them without reference to others. Organizations have authority, too. They can declare the business they are in, establish goals and strategies, and execute them.

One way to understand how the matter of authority affects organizational life is to draw a vertical line through the middle of the three overlapping circles of the Enabling Leader model, as shown in *Figure 9*. You can then begin to see where this balance lies. The left-hand side of the line represents those things that are the concern of the organization: its needs, aims and objectives. On this side of the line, the organization has authority. When you join an organization, you sign up to that authority.

The area on the right-hand side of the line represents those things that are the concern of individuals: their needs, aims and objectives. On this side of the line, individuals have authority.

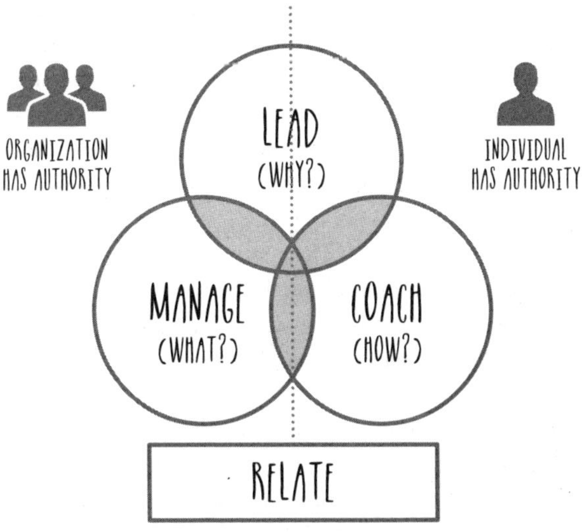

FIGURE 9 **THE ELEMENTS OF THE TEAM LEADER'S ROLE, CLASSIFIED ACCORDING TO AUTHORITY**

It is overly simplistic but nevertheless useful shorthand to suggest that *what* an individual employee does sits on the left-hand side in the authority of the organization. Clearly, this is best agreed – with the manager using coaching skills to understand the individual – rather than decreed. *How* the *what* gets executed sits for the most part on the right-hand side of the line, in the authority of the individual employee.

We can draw a parallel with the game of tennis. When a player stands on a tennis court, they implicitly sign up to the rules of the game as laid down by the International Tennis Federation. The player cannot change the size of the court or the height of the net, or alter the rules. They cannot, for instance, decide to kick the ball. If they do, the game ceases to be tennis.

In addition to the player, there are a number of other people on the tennis court: the opponent, the umpire and the coach. The umpire and the coach are of interest in this analogy, not the opponent. The umpire's role is essentially about compliance. It is their job to ensure that the rules of the game are adhered to. In this sense, their job is analogous to the management element of the team manager's role.

The coach's role is different. Their job is to ensure that the player gives their best performance and learns and improves from one match to the next. This is obviously analogous to the coaching aspect of the team leader's role.

The very different roles of the umpire and the coach suggest different kinds of relationship with the player, and different corresponding behaviours. The umpire's relationship is invested with authority, as decreed by the governing body. It is a directive, command and-control, interactive style – and appropriately so, for if the rules were not enforced, there would be no game.

The coach's relationship with the player is altogether different. The conversations between the coach and the player concern matters that are within the authority of the player: whether they hit a backhand with one or two hands on the racket, or whether they adopt an aggressive serve-and-volley strategy or a backcourt, counter-hitting approach.

On the right-hand side of the diagram, where the individual has authority, instructing or telling that individual is less effective than listening to them and asking questions such that they come to their own solution or insight. This is the fundamental reason why coaching is predominantly a following interest activity.

The word 'authority' can give us an insight here. It has the same Latin root as the word 'author': a writer, someone who creates. The root is *auctus*, which means, among other things, to produce, to increase or to cause to grow their own book. Having someone dictating the book to be written would soon wear the patience of the writer, turning them into a mere scribe, thus destroying their motivation and, in time, their very ability to be creative. Effective team leaders invest in the authority – the capacity to produce, to create – of the team members.

In organizations that adhere to traditional ways of doing things, the failure to distinguish between managing and coaching elements of the team leader's role causes a kind of leakage. Team leaders try to handle performance and learning with a command-and-control approach rather than a more facilitative approach designed to align and enable. This leakage derives from the fact that, for most people, those they have encountered who have been charged with helping them to perform or learn effectively have also had a management responsibility.

Teachers teach, but they also ensure discipline in the class and at certain times pass judgement on their pupils' efforts – judgements that dictate the immediate future. This is true for team leaders, too. And, for the most part, neither professional has recognized that the style appropriate to their teaching or coaching works less well for their disciplinary and evaluative activities. One leaks into the other. The umpire and the coach in the tennis analogy have it easier, as the roles are split between them; the team leader, however, has to wear both hats.

There is a school of thought that proposes 'managing with a coaching style.' Many books and articles have been written around variations on the idea of 'the manager as coach.' This is another form of leakage. In one company that we know of, it is almost impossible for a team leader to give a direct instruction to a member of staff – they have to coach. This is just clumsy or incomplete thinking, and it can have the effect of undermining the team leader. It is important to separate one circle from the other.

Interestingly, when we distinguish between the two sides of the vertical line, the management element takes up less time; when you place authority where it mostly belongs – with the individual – the need to manage diminishes. It does not go away, but it takes less time.

There is, it seems, a somewhat worrying corollary of this. Some years ago, Myles ran a workshop for the UK management team of a well-known fast-food chain with the intent of introducing them to coaching. The workshop was difficult; there was a level of polite engagement but no passion, which is unusual. It was only afterwards, when Myles reflected on the event, that he saw what had happened. From their perspective, there was only one way to cook a burger – quality (if that is what you call it) and consistency were everything. The 'shop-floor' culture – one of managing, not coaching – had engulfed the leadership team.

Clearly, if there is little or no need to coach, there should be little or no coaching; in some jobs, standardization is the key to success. The problem for the fast-food chain was that away from the shop floor, the leadership style had become very directive, resulting in a culture where risk was avoided and innovation suppressed. It is difficult for such a business to diversify.

These ideas on authority also relate to the third circle of the Enabling Manager model – Lead – where the line down the middle retains its validity. Sometimes, it will be appropriate for a leader to make a clear and unequivocal statement about a direction to take, or to make a difficult decision without referring to others. At other times, the leader may adopt a more facilitative, coaching approach to a leadership issue and elicit a decision from others.

In summary, there are a number of issues to bear in mind:

- Team leaders need to lead: to keep present in the minds of their team members the overarching aims of the organization, and be role models for the desired values and behaviours
- Team leaders need to manage, and have a responsibility to both their team members and the organization to do so
- Team leaders – as part of managing – need to agree clear goals for their direct reports; interestingly, while this is clearly a management task, using coaching skills to identify the goals in the first case is always more effective
- Team leaders need to hold their direct reports to account for the goals that have been agreed
- Once the goals have been agreed, and any other parameters surrounding the role (such as values and behaviours), the team leader needs to coach their team members to achieve the agreed goals

Team leadership that embraces Lead – Manage – Coach can help to create flow (see *Chapter 3*) and the holy grail of high performance.

Using coaching as part of your skill set

Using coaching as part of your skill set does not require a clear agreement from your team. The skills can be used on the spur of the moment. In the canteen, a colleague indicates that they are having a difficult time with a particular client or with some aspect of a project; a member of staff complains that they will never get the job done on time. Both of these are opportunities to coach.

In some of our workshops we get the participants to pair up and to give three-minute coaching sessions. They are always surprised at how much can be achieved in such a short space of time.

This three-minute exercise was developed with a client in the United States – an international strategic management consultancy – where the only coaching that individuals got from their partner (manager) occurred as they held open the door of a taxi. We exaggerate, a little. Could the time be used more effectively? Yes, we called it 'kerbside coaching' originally, then thought better of it and now we call it 'corridor coaching.'

It can be as simple as asking four questions – and listening to the response:

> "What do you want to discuss?"
> "What else do I need to know?"
> "What could you do?"
> "What are you going to do?"

Clearly, a three-minute conversation is not suitable for all topics, but using short spaces of time effectively can make a big difference. As the HR director of an international beverage producer and distributor observed: "This is not about Innovation with a capital 'I' in our business but rather about hundreds and hundreds of innovations – small 'i' – all across the organization, in every conversation."

Coaching your team members

Most organizations have a number of management processes that lend themselves to coaching, in particular such people-management processes as performance reviews, appraisals, development reviews, objective-setting meetings and progress reviews. It staggers us that there are still organizations where the team leaders set development goals for their team members. We can't think of many quicker or more sure-fire ways to erode motivation and undermine responsibility.

Thankfully, most modern organizations are more enlightened than that, and allow for self-assessment and for employees to identify their own goals. Both of these processes provide perfect opportunities to wrap coaching around management processes. Think about the really critical conversations – the ones that have a significant impact in organizations: conversations to set objectives, to agree budgets, to establish or review projects. Now imagine if these conversations were redesigned as coaching conversations.

Take the budgeting process. A team member is sent off to prepare a budget. After a while, they come back with their best effort and are told to strip out 10% of the costs – and what about the new product launch? There's another iteration, and probably another. In this process, time is wasted, enthusiasm is eroded, and the relationship between team leader and team member is undermined. And there is little or no learning.

With effective coaching, up-front, this would be less likely to occur, thus providing a great boost to organizational effectiveness.

Lead – Manage – Coach during major change

Among the most debilitating side effects of major change – be it organizational or cultural – are fear and uncertainty. These result in large numbers of people looking for answers to an array of questions, usually from the leadership group.

Adopting Lead – Manage – Coach as a way of working has a number of benefits. Firstly, it has the effect of putting ownership and control back into the hands of the team members, and this can lessen anxiety. Secondly, in change situations, where there are often no right answers, coaching will draw out possibilities and options from which the best can be selected. Thirdly, it gives some respite to the leaders, as others begin to take responsibility and join in the game. Leaders can't – and shouldn't – do it all.

Before and after training events

Lead – Manage – Coach can be used to great effect to ensure that someone gets full value from a training programme. The team leader can communicate the business objectives for the programme and coach a delegate prior to an event so that they are very clear about their learning objectives. When the event is completed, a further conversation can consolidate the learning and ensure that it is effectively applied in the workplace.

Enabling leadership in your team

When there is alignment between what inspires an individual, the job they are doing and the direction of the organization, people at all levels can give their best freely, communication becomes easier and phenomenal results can be achieved. Lead – Manage – Coach directly involves staff in the direction the business takes, and the shape of individuals' jobs can be part of what creates that alignment.

Lead – Manage – Coach can also be used to enable people to understand how organizational values and behaviours will work out in their roles and, in this way, help them to own them. For instance, working with someone to identify their own values and then helping them to relate these to the organization's values – and therefore discovering which elements are congruent and which are not – will bring the values to life in a meaningful way, particularly if there is room for debate (and influencing) around those elements where there is discomfort.

Coaching upward

"Is it possible to coach my boss?" is a question frequently asked at coaching skills workshops. The answer is that anyone can be coached – if they are willing. What is interesting, we think, is what is behind the question. Usually, the underlying question is, "How can I change my boss's behaviour?" To this question there is a different answer: you cannot change anyone else's behaviour – only they can.

Using your coaching skills in conversations with your boss is possible but is dependent on the prevailing culture within the organization – and on just how much of a control junkie the person 'upward' of you is.

Mentoring

The models, tools and skills of Lead – Manage – Coach will also make a more effective mentor. A mentor who is reliant on having had significant experience of the organization, business and life may well provide great benefit and be a wonderful person to be around. A mentor who has vast experience and can use it to good effect – and who can also employ a following interest approach when appropriate – will have a much greater impact.

A THOUGHT EXPERIMENT TO TRY

Think about your life, both at work and outside of work. Consider the following questions:

- What difference do you like to make to people's lives?
- What do you do that enables you to make this difference?
- How does that benefit your organization?
- What would need to happen to allow you to do more of this?
- How would it change the way you felt about your work?

WANT TO KNOW MORE?

Identity Economics: How Our Identities Shape Our Work, Wages, and Well-Being
by George Akerlof and Rachel Kranton[48]
This book introduces a new branch of behavioural economics. The authors demonstrate how our sense of identity informs the choices we make at home, at work and at school. The research underlines the importance of enabling members of your team to feel recognized and valued for who they are.

CHAPTER 13

Developing Your Team

Part of your responsibilities as a team leader is to develop your team and to ensure that the team performs as an effective unit, achieving its collective goals.

Many organizations have invested time and money in developing teamwork in the hope that it will increase performance. No doubt there will have been some benefit to the bottom line in some cases, but the vast majority of team-building and team-development exercises flounder when the raft they have built hits the rapids. Such approaches almost never translate into the workplace, and 'high-performance teams' become so dependent on 'process' – doing it the right way – that individuals' needs and the task itself are left behind. Of course, there are exceptions. But in the main, the learning – such as it is – is not sustainable. As a team leader your role is to ensure that the team achieves its goals. Any activity or exercise that the team undertakes must contribute to this and thus the organization's goals.

The most obvious distinction between working with individuals and working with teams is the number of people involved. At the surface level, this means that using Lead – Manage – Coach requires more time when you are working with teams. An individual can get to a level of clarity and make a decision relatively quickly. In a team, the same process takes much more time, as each person needs to be heard, disagreement needs to be handled, and consensus and commitment need to be built. When you look below the surface, you see the interrelationships in the team, including its dynamics and evolution, and a whole new ball game emerges.

These issues should not scare you off choosing to use your coaching skills with the whole team because, as will become evident, there is an inherent resource unique to teams that can produce a form of 'self-coaching.' This resource is the very human desire to be in communion. In this state, a team can achieve extraordinary goals with minimal effort.

This chapter, then, is about the inner aspect of teams. We'll identify some of the interferences (see *Chapter 3*) that can occur in teams and suggest a number of ways of eliminating them.

The inner aspects of teams

Tim Gallwey's initial explorations of the inner game concerned individuals and identified the extraordinary capacity of human beings to get in their own way – self-interference. He observed that the single greatest factor that inhibits performance is human doubt.[49] In a group situation, doubt is contagious, and as it grips it deepens – ultimately into panic. In a team, interference is multiplied – no, squared – and, in the worst cases, performance diminishes to the point where one person could do the work of the team in a fraction of the time.

The purpose of creating and maintaining a team is to achieve higher performance. For a team to experience more of its potential, the interference must be reduced. Interference in a team might include the following:

- Lack of trust in other team members
- Fear of ridicule
- Fear of being dominated
- Pursuit of personal agendas
- Need to lead
- Lack of clarity about the task or goals
- Pursuit of incongruent goals
- Hidden agendas
- Not understanding (or distrusting) each other's intentions
- No agreed process for working together
- Absence of agreed ground rules
- Rivalries
- No listening
- No meaningful collective work
- Entrenched beliefs and positions ("this is how things are or should be")

A team that is successful in reducing the interference will be characterized by the following:

- Apparent absence of hierarchy in relationships
- Listening and a desire to understand each other

- Robust, challenging conversations
- Seeking and giving of clear feedback
- Pursuit of 'impossible' goals
- Focused activity
- Intuitive sense of what each member is focused on and how they are doing
- Requests for, and offers of, help or support
- Flexibility about roles and a willingness to cover for each other
- Creativity, imagination and intuition
- Team members caring for each other and each other's well-being
- Fun, joy and the simple pleasure of being together
- Silence and thoughtfulness before decisions and action
- Mutual accountability for the achievement of goals

You may have noticed the correlation between the interference factors – and those characterizing their absence – and the conditions of flow as described in *Chapter 3*.

Considered from this perspective, your role as a team leader is, in part, to help the team to reduce the interference and to achieve a shared mental state, or 'team think' as we call it.

The big three

There are three top-of-the-list, most-wanted elements of successful teamwork. If these are not present, the most massive interference is unleashed. We realize that stating them baldly here is almost prosaic, bordering on the self-evident, but our experience is that people don't see them – and this blindness means that failure is imminent. These three elements are *who*, *what* and *how*.

When a group of people come together to perform a task, each individual needs to understand *who* each person in the team is, *what* the task is and *how* they are going to contribute to achieving it. The degree to which these things are not clear is the degree to which effectiveness is diminished.

In this context, to understand '*who* each person is' means to have sufficient insight into them such that they can be trusted and their intentions are clear. The *what* means that there is clarity about the task facing the group: why are they doing it, and what would success look like?

Interestingly, 'task' must be understood at two levels:

- Level one is the final output – the result, the goal
- Level two is what needs to be done immediately next in order to move efficiently toward the level-one goal

An example of level two would be when a team needs to address a relationship issue in the group before they can discuss what might be a more obvious level-one issue, such as a matter of strategy. If the team fails to address the relationship issue, they will certainly come unstuck when they discuss the strategy. The interference will block their capacity to have a meaningful, creative conversation – or, worse still, some people, whose buy-in may be critical, may simply sit on the sidelines and at a later date claim they were never in agreement.

How is about the process of achieving the level-one aims. It concerns a wide spectrum of activities, from strategy and priorities to communication, meeting frequency, agendas and ground rules.

The degree to which these elements need to be clear, understood and agreed upon is dictated by the difficulty of the task. A group meeting to decide the allocation of car-parking spaces does not need the same level of insight and clarity into *who*, *what* and *how* as one about a team responsible for the rapid construction of a £300 million factory.

Reducing interference in teams

The ideas expressed below are intended to give you a sense of how to reduce interference in teams. This list is neither comprehensive nor exhaustive, and the exercises within can be made more sophisticated. Here we just want you to get the idea.

CREATING A COMMON VISION (*WHAT*)

Creating a common vision or set of goals can help to reduce interference in as much as it is tangible evidence that everyone in the team is on the same side. The creation of the vision may also flush out disagreements about the direction the team is taking. A discussion early on in the life of the team that sorts out such differences reduces internal bickering and upset.

Creating a common vision can be approached in hundreds of ways. The simplest is to get each individual to write down their vision or goals and then read them out to the team. Other members of the team listen and, when the readings are complete, you ask the team to identify the common points and themes. The advantage of starting with the personal visions is that the disclosures begin to generate understanding, and therefore relationships, within the team.

AGREEING A MODUS OPERANDI (*HOW*)

Once the vision and goals have been agreed, the team needs to discuss how they will achieve them. The potential for friction within the team can be greatly reduced by creating an agreement about how the individuals will cooperate. The question for the team leader to ask here is: "What are the ground rules that would support this team in achieving its goals?"

Start capturing the suggestions on a flip chart without engaging in debate or assessment. When the team has run out of suggestions, ask them to select those ground rules to which they are all committed. These should be reviewed at subsequent meetings and can obviously be changed, added to or removed. Ground rules might include agreements about the function and frequency of team meetings, the values that they will adhere to (honesty, respect and so on), and when the team will make decisions by unanimity, by consensus or when it will be the team leader's decision.

DISCLOSURE OF LIFE AND CAREER GOALS (*WHO*)

This is a very simple team exercise and can even be done over a meal or a drink. Give the team members some time to prepare and think through their goals individually – to do it properly, you may even want to work with the individual team members prior to the meeting. The individuals then talk together as a team about their personal goals. This exercise works because it builds understanding and therefore trust.

FACILITATING FEEDBACK (*WHO*, BUT CAN DRAG UP ISSUES OF *WHAT* AND *HOW*)

We have already spoken about feedback in *Chapter 10*. Again, this exercise should build understanding and trust in the group. The simplest method is for each team member to take a turn in the 'hot chair.' The other members of the team then give individual feedback.

Giving a standard format to the feedback can make this easier. For example:

- One thing I would like you to stop doing is …
- One thing I would like you to start doing is …
- One thing I would like you to continue doing is …

IDENTIFICATION OF INTERNAL AND EXTERNAL OBSTACLES (*WHO*, *WHAT* AND *HOW*)

This exercise is a way of getting the team to identify the interference for itself. There is more ownership this way. The question to ask the team is this: "What are the obstacles, within the team or outside the team, to being successful or achieving your vision?" Note down all the obstacles on a flip chart and ask the team to rank them in order of their impact on the team. You can then use the GROW model (see *Chapter 7*) to resolve the issues, thus reducing interference.

SURFACING CONFLICT

There will almost always be a tendency to avoid conflict, in life and in teams. If this happens, the team is stuck and no meaningful work can be done. As the team leader, your role is to notice the conflict when it rears its head and to ensure that the team talk it through. Arranging for the parties in conflict to clearly state their positions is the first step. Ensuring that each opposing party listens is the second.

An option here is to get each party to state the opposing party's position. You also need to check that the relationships survive intact – or, better still, deepen – following the conflict. Questioning each party about how they feel about each other is a good starting point.

When a team is in conflict and is not making progress, try calling it out and declaring one minute of silence. This is a very challenging and powerful technique. The reflection that the individuals engage in during this minute is undistracted and seems to bring them face to face with their integrity. At the end of the silence, someone will usually take the risk and say what needs to be said, thus unblocking the team.

Achieving 'team think'

'Team think' is how we describe a state in which team members are so aware of each other and take such care of each other that they are coaching themselves. The state of team think is achievable, but it requires some effort. However, even making progress on the road to team think pays immediate and noticeable dividends.

There is some really good news about building a team, and specifically about reducing interference: most people want to be in relationships with those around them. And they want the relationships to be meaningful. Of course, they may have to unlearn some things before they can have those relationships, but at least as a team leader you should know that, in this sense at least, you are working *with* gravity and not against it.

There is something instinctive at work that guides people toward greater union. We do not particularly want to get spiritual about this, but we guess it is a higher expression of what we are as human beings.

Using the GROW model in team meetings

Using the GROW model in team meetings can help in a number of ways. Each item of the agenda can be discussed using the GROW model. In this way, you can ensure that for each item of the agenda, there is a clear and agreed outcome, a robust shared understanding of the subject, and agreed and measurable next steps. The benefits are:

- It will keep the meeting focused
- It will enable all options to be explored
- It will ensure actionable outcomes
- It will prevent you from turning up with all the answers

The big picture

In a team meeting that has been called to address a single issue, you can treat the whole meeting as a single conversation that you shape around the GROW model:

T: What is the meeting about?
G: What outcomes do we want from this meeting?
R: What is the current situation? (This may lead to identifying separate issues that need to be addressed during the meeting. In this case, each item on the agenda can become its own GROW conversation.)
O: What could we do?
W: What will we do? Who will do it? When will they do it? What support do they need?

Using the Model T in teams

The concept of 'following interest' (see *Chapter 6*) in teams may be difficult to grasp, with so many different and potentially divergent agendas. The Model T, originally introduced in *Chapter 7*, proves to be a magnificently powerful technique in this situation.

The model says that you expand before you focus, and in this way you ensure that you hear everyone who has something to say. Once everyone's thoughts are on the table, you can lead a group discussion on where to focus your attention. In this way, everyone feels valued and you can draw out contributions from those who are more reflective or slower to share their thoughts.

Teamwork: a summary

The whole issue of teamwork is so huge that this chapter can only serve as an introduction. We hope, however, that it will enable you to make a start – and a difference – by thinking about your role as a team leader through the lens of Lead – Manage – Coach. The key is to get started. You can only be the team leader you are capable of being by getting on and doing the work.

A PRACTICAL EXPERIMENT TO TRY

Next time you are preparing for a team meeting, use the GROW model:

T: What is the meeting about?

G: What is the goal of the meeting?

R: What is the reality of the current situation? How could you make sure you understand everyone's perspectives?

O: What different ways could you lead the meeting?

W: What are you going to do? What needs to be done before the meeting? How will you lead the meeting?

WANT TO KNOW MORE?

Tribal Leadership: Leveraging Natural Groups to Build a Thriving Organization by Dave Logan, John King and Halee Fischer-Wright[50]
A fascinating and unique look at the ways in which 'tribes' form within organizations. The authors provide practical ways of identifying five different levels of tribe and suggest ways of moving people into higher levels of engagement and performance.

The Different Drum by M. Scott Peck[51]
Although we have developed the technology to make communication more efficient and to bring people closer together, we have failed to use it to build a true global community. This radical and challenging book describes how communities work, how group action can be developed on the principles of tolerance and love, and how we can start to transform world society into a true community.

"Developmental Sequence in Small Groups" by Bruce Tuckman[52]
You may have heard group development described in terms of "forming, norming, storming and performing." These stages were proposed by Bruce Tuckman in 1965. For those who want to do a deep dive into group dynamics, this is a great place to start.

CHAPTER 14

Becoming an Enabling Leader: The Foundations

Becoming an enabling leader or manager requires you to have thought through two key questions: What do you want from your team? And how do you as an individual need to turn up?

In this book, we have focused on the skills that you can work on to become the kind of team leader who enables people to be part of an effective and productive team. The same skills should also help you enable them to succeed above and beyond standard norms over the long term. But using these skills we have spoken about also requires you to explore your potential as a leader.

Understand your intent

As you think through how to put the ideas in this book into practice, it is helpful to think about the context in which you will be using them. One way of approaching this is to think about your intent as a team leader (both now and in the future). What is it that your role requires? What outcomes do you want, or need, to achieve?

We can think about the intent of a team leader under three broad headings, each of which entails a type of response from the team members:

- **Compliance:** you simply need your team to follow instructions and do a job of work
- **Engagement:** you want a team that owns their work, feels valued for their contribution and is bought-in to delivering the business goals
- **Thriving or flow:** the foundation of high performance; the vision we described in *Chapter 3*

Whatever your intent, you will need good relationships with your team and you will need to use the skills of Lead – Manage – Coach. If your intent is simply to achieve compliance, then coaching may play a relatively small part in your leadership. If, on the other hand, you want to build a team that is engaged and able to access higher levels of performance, then you will need to make increasing use of your coaching skills.

A good place to start when considering your intent is to step back and think about the kind of leader you want to be. How do you want to turn up? One helpful way of thinking about this is to think in terms of will, love and desire.

Will is the capacity to have desires and to act intentionally toward achieving them:

- Will is 'head' (rational and intellectual) while love is 'heart' (intuitive)
- Will seeks control whereas love trusts and lets it happen
- Will looks for structure whereas love seeks process

Love is so many things to so many people that we are not going to risk a definition – or write a poem, which, other than songs, seems to be the most common route to understanding and communicating about it. Not something for this book! However, it is accurate to suggest that love's fundamental function is to bring people together for a variety of purposes: procreation, nurturing and acting together for the common good, either to protect against threats or to achieve a collective aim, such as growing a crop or hunting.

These two basic human attributes – will and love – can be seen as being in competition with each other. From this perspective, the solution is to find a compromise. But there is another way of approaching them and that is to bring them together in a synthesis. To do this, we need to look at something in us that operates at a higher level, something that transcends will and love but that harnesses them both. That function can be fulfilled by our desires. 'Love' often defines our desires but 'will' enables us to do what is required to realize them (see *Figure 10*).

True desire is congruent with our sense of identity, our sense of self and our sense of purpose. It embraces the best of will and the best of love. It is persistent and endures over time; it flexes in the face of changes in circumstance, and it is a primary source of energy. Desire emerges from within; it is primarily an intrinsic motivation.

FIGURE 10 **DESIRE, WILL AND LOVE**

What we want (desire) from a situation changes the way love and will turn up in our attitudes and actions. A team leader who wants to be 'in control' and 'in charge' will turn up in a way in which their will is dominant. A team leader who wants to be 'liked' will turn up in a way in which love is dominant. If leadership is all will and no love, then it will be domineering and very definitely in the realm of command and control. On the other hand, if leadership is all love and no will, then you may form a close-knit group of friends but there will be no direction. Effective team leaders turn up with a combination of love and will that enables them to realize what they want their team to achieve.

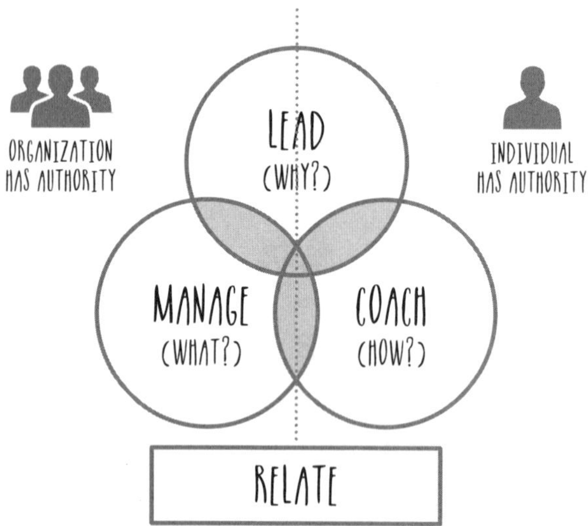

FIGURE 11 **A REMINDER OF THE ENABLING LEADER MODEL, SHOWING THE BALANCE BETWEEN ORGANIZATIONAL AND INDIVIDUAL AUTHORITY**

With that in mind, think about the Enabling Leader model and the way it can be thought of in terms of authority, as shown in *Figure 11*. The whole model is built (and only works) on a foundation of good relationships, which require a healthy balance of love and will:

- **Lead** maps roughly onto the concept of desire. Leadership speaks to what the business wants and aligns those desires with what employees want out of their work.
- **Manage** maps roughly onto the concept of will. Management concerns itself with *what* people must do. It creates and enforces processes and procedures. It is about getting stuff done in the right way and at the right time.
- **Coach** maps roughly onto the idea of love. It is about engaging with individuals. It expresses the value that you as a leader place in their skills, creativity and insights. It gives them autonomy and expresses trust.

We began this chapter by encouraging you to consider your intent. When you bring this together with the ideas of desire, love and will, you can begin to think about the leader you want to be. Consider:

- What is your intent for your team (compliance, engagement or thriving)?
- What is the balance of love and will required to get the best out of your team?

Becoming an enabling leader

In *Chapter 2* we took some time to think about entrepreneurial leadership and the mission command approach of the US military. We identified four things they have in common:

- Recognition of, and trust in, the capability of each individual member of the team
- The role of leadership in determining the desired outcomes
- The role of leadership to clearly communicate the business's vision and goals, and the role of individuals and teams in achieving them
- Recognition of the freedom of individuals and teams to determine what they need to do to achieve their objectives

If we take these four ideas, we can construct a four-step guide to becoming an enabling leader.

STEP 1: BUILD TRUST

One key to building trust is open and honest communication. When people detect a hidden agenda or feel like they are in the dark, they become suspicious and start to protect themselves. In our experience, communication – or lack of it – is one of the biggest issues faced by many businesses.

Team members need to believe in one another's positive intentions. None of us get things right all the time but mistakes are much easier to address when we start with an assumption that they were honest mistakes – the wrong thing done for the right reasons.

Demonstrate respect for the insights, skills and expertise of each member of your team. You'll find it is catching, and people in the team will develop respect for each other.

When we talk with people about trusting positive intentions and respecting others' skills and expertise, it is not long before someone asks the question: "What if they don't deserve it?" The answer to that question is a little brutal, but first it leads us to another important part of building trust.

Constant feedback and the ability to challenge each other are vital for your team to function at its best. Good teams hold each other accountable. The people in your team were employed because it was believed that they had what it took to do the work well. If we start with respect and a belief in people's positive intentions, then everything we say flows from an expression of trust. We can reinforce that trust by acknowledging people's successes and making sure they understand how valued they are. We can also challenge their thoughts or actions without diminishing how much we value them.

There will of course be people who oversell themselves in interviews or who develop intransigent attitudes or behaviours that undermine our trust and prevent us from believing that their intentions are positive. To put it bluntly, your job as a team leader is to help them to understand that they would be better off seeking a position elsewhere.

STEP 2: GET CLARITY ON YOUR BUSINESS OBJECTIVES

Having clarity about the objectives of the business enables you to define the field of play and the objectives of the game. Only when you have clarity on why the business does what it does and what the business is trying to achieve can you create the context in which your team can be set free to do what they do best.

STEP 3: TAKE TIME TO UNDERSTAND HOW EACH PERSON IN YOUR TEAM CONTRIBUTES TO ACHIEVING YOUR BUSINESS OBJECTIVES

We often find that team leaders who know what the business is trying to achieve can't explain how the people in their team contribute to those objectives. People slip into doing what they do because it is what they do and because they are asked or expected to do it. It is your role to enable people to connect their activity with the purpose of the business so that they understand how they contribute, feel valued and can make better decisions.

STEP 4: ENABLE YOUR TEAM TO DETERMINE HOW THEY ARE GOING TO ACHIEVE THE RESULTS YOU NEED

We have spent large parts of this book discussing how to use coaching skills in conversations with your team. Having created clarity about *why* your team does what it does and *what* it is that you need them to deliver, as an enabling leader you must step back and use coaching skills to enable people to use their skills, insights and expertise to determine *how* they will deliver the desired outcomes.

A PRACTICAL EXPERIMENT TO TRY

Work through this chapter as an exercise to better understand your own leadership style.

What do you need to do next to continue to grow and develop as a team leader?

WANT TO KNOW MORE?

The Act of Will by Roberto Assagioli[53]

This is a rewarding (though not easy) read. It addresses a central theme of psychosynthesis (i.e. the relationship between the person and the self). Assagioli acknowledges personal will as an essential function of human beings and altruistic love as an expression of the will of self.

Mindset: The New Psychology of Success by Carol Dweck[54]

This is the book that popularized the idea of a 'Growth Mindset.' It is a must-read if you want to dig deeper into understanding why some people are able to continue learning and growing while others get stuck.

CHAPTER 15

Discovering Your Own Genius for Leadership

You bring a unique personality to your leadership, shaped by your own unique background. No one else will lead quite like you do. It is time to discover your unique genius for leadership.

Identity has many guises. People ask at a party, "What do you do?" They try to place your accent. Try to establish whether you are married. Your sexuality. Your age. Your religion. Your wealth. Your place in society. All in order to find out something about who you are.

The easy thing to say in this chapter would be "just be yourself" but from our observations, that's not always a good idea!

When people tell us to be ourselves, we often let it slip past us as if we know what it means. If we are feeling insecure, perhaps in a new environment or role, we may find ourselves wondering: what does it mean? When we ask that question, we suddenly discover how unhelpful the comment is. What is this 'self' that we talk about?

Probably the most common view of the self is that there is a something buried deep inside of us – a pearl – that defines us. If you're religious, you may associate this with the idea of having a soul. The problem is, whether you call it a soul or not, this view doesn't get us any closer to understanding ourselves – and, from a purely physical and neurological point of view, no one has ever found this pearl.

Another view of the self is to think of it as a construct – a mental model you build from your biology, your environment, your experiences, your memories and the way others have responded to you. All these things become part of how you think about yourself – a bundle of things rather than a unified pearl. Unconsciously, you are constructing a sense of identity. Your sense of self is not a fixed reality that you are born with and have to work around. It is an interpretation of your experience of life. It is also essential to our emergence as individual human beings.

All of this suggests that, as time passes or circumstances change, you can reinvent yourself. Reinventions most obviously occur as people pass through different ages and stages in their lives. The mother who brought up the children goes back to work. The former executive takes on a non-executive directorship and a role in a charity. As your experience grows and changes, you discover new things about yourself and come to think of yourself in a different way.

Back in 2016 we brought together a team to spend some time answering two questions:

- What is genius?
- Is it possible to enable genius in ourselves and others?

The result of the team's work was the book *Enabling Genius* – which might give you a clue about our conclusions. We came up with five propositions:

1. Genius is available to all
2. Each person can develop a unique individual genius
3. Each person can develop a unique genius in any discipline, craft or skill
4. Moments of genius are available to all
5. People can work together in a state of collective genius[55]

It is the second proposition that is of most interest here. Touching lightly on the first, the optimal way of developing your unique individual genius is to work out what you're naturally good at (nature) and develop that (nurture). And so we would argue that you have a unique individual genius and that, in line with the second proposition, you also have a unique genius as a leader.

Once you understand what your unique genius is, you can develop it. You can also work out the strategies and tactics that flow from that genius and way of being. From this base we perform, learn, promote ourselves and take our place in the world.

Roger Federer and Rafael Nadal, two of the greatest tennis players of all time, know precisely who they are, on the court at least. On the foundation of a clear identity, they have each built their unique approach to playing the game. One is completely different from the other, but both are real and authentic. Their identities give rise to and define their individual strategies and tactics, and inform what they need to learn and develop.

As an example of how everyone can develop their own unique individual genius in any discipline, some years ago Myles needed to put more attention on his sales activities after a period of writing. In thinking about this, he realized that his internal approach needed to shift as writing requires a different energy to selling. He asked himself a series of questions to see if he could identify his sales genius and bring 'him' to life. The questions included:

- What's his name?
- What kind of energy does he have?
- What is his dominant attitude?
- What music does he listen to?
- How does he dress?

If the last question seems a little shallow, then it is important to understand that our minds respond to how we present ourselves. During the Covid-19 pandemic, many office-based workers found themselves working from home. Many of them had dreamt about the opportunity and now it was reality. The dream had come true – they could work in their pyjamas if they so wished. If they had a Zoom call, they could put a nice top on and sit in their joggers – nobody would know.

It turns out that the most important person did know. For the first few days (maybe weeks), working in your pyjamas is a novelty – you feel relaxed and can be quite productive. However, as the novelty wears off, the relaxed productivity slowly turns into an unfocused, distracted lack of motivation. The solution – get up and dress for work. It changes your mindset, you are more focused and you recover your productivity. How you dress and your posture may sometimes reflect your mood but they can also inform your mood. It works both ways.

For Myles, this exercise wasn't about becoming someone different but about understanding who he was in his sales role. It worked – Myles found new energy with which to pursue his sales goals. He also clarified his approach so that he was more focused and therefore closer to being in flow (see *Chapter 3*) when in sales situations.

Take some time to reflect on your different roles: at work, at home and in the community. Notice how you turn up to each of those roles. We're confident that what you will find is that without becoming a different person, you turn up in different ways in different contexts. Depending on the role you are fulfilling, different parts of your personality will come to the foreground. Identifying and developing the different ways you show up is key to being successful.

Your unique individual genius as a leader

We firmly believe that you are capable of approaching your role as a team leader with a genius that is unique to you. At the risk of sounding a bit too clichéd, there is only one person who has the unique combination of nature and nurture that makes you who you are. No one else could approach leading your team quite like you do.

In the same way that Myles was able to improve his sales activities by identifying who he was in his sales role, you can improve your leadership by getting clear about who you want to be and how you want to show up as a team leader.

Developing your identity as a team leader also helps to build trust with your team. In order to have a relationship with you, your team members need to have a sense of who you are. They need to get a handle on you as a leader. This means that they can have some certainty about the person who shows up from day to day and can feel confident making plans and agreements with you.

Here is an exercise that will get you started in thinking about what your unique genius might look like.

Imagine you have called a team meeting to brief everyone on an upcoming project (or to inform everyone about an important change):

- What are your aims in this meeting?
- What do you need to get out of this meeting?
- To achieve these aims and get the outcomes you need, what attributes of your personality do you need to use?

Now look at the meeting from the point of view of a member of your team. Put yourself in their shoes:

- What are their aims for the meeting?
- What do they need to get out of the meeting?
- To achieve these aims and to get these outcomes, what do they need from their team leader?

Finally, look at the meeting from the point of view of an observer. Imagine yourself able to see and hear everything that is going on. You can hear yourself address the team, you can see the body language around the room, and you can hear the questions and responses of the team. Consider:

- What do you notice?
- What would the team leader need to do to improve their leadership and get better results from the team?
    - What feedback would you give them on what you thought went well and what they could have done differently?
    - What energy would they need to bring to the room?
    - What parts of their personality got the most productive responses?
    - How could they have communicated better?

This next exercise gives you another approach to try.

Think about how you would describe what a great team leader looks like in your organization or industry. Reflect on the way they think about themselves, the way they interact with their team, what they do and how they say things. You might even like to think about how they dress or their physical posture. Make your description as rich and as full as you can. Once you have your description, ask yourself the following questions:

- How do I need to think about myself in my role?
- How do I need to interact with my team to enable them to be the best they can be?
- What do I need to do to be a great team leader?
- How do I need to communicate with my team?
- What clothes will make me feel like the leader I want to be?
- How do I need to hold myself physically to feel like the leader I want to be?

We'll end with an exercise you can do every day.

Begin your day by looking at what you need to achieve by the time you go to bed. Ask yourself: what three attributes do I need to be the best I can be today? Write them down on a slip of paper. Then, on a scale of 1 to 10, rate yourself on how well you are demonstrating those attributes. Slip the paper into a pocket or into your bag and get on with your day. At lunchtime rate yourself again. Finally, toward the end of the day, give yourself a final rating between 1 and 10. More often than not, without paying conscious attention to the three attributes you identified, you will find that your ratings improve through the day. Remember – awareness is curative.

A final note

There is no set recipe for being a great team leader. Every leader is unique. At your best, no one else will be quite like you in the way you lead your team, and the people in your team are all the better for that fact.

Leadership is a craft that is learned with practice. The basic skills are easily taught but they are mastered with practice. We are confident that as you use the skills of Lead – Manage – Coach, and as you discover your own unique genius for leadership, you can become a great team leader. You can be the kind of leader who provides a context for your team to use their insights, skills and expertise to achieve great things together. And, in this context, people will achieve great things, find their work fulfilling and enjoy turning up.

A PRACTICAL EXPERIMENT TO TRY

Through this chapter we set out a number of exercises to help you identify your unique genius as a team leader. If you have not already done so, take time now to go back through the chapter completing each of the exercises.

WANT TO KNOW MORE?

Enabling Genius: A Mindset for Success in the 21st Century by Myles Downey[56]

From 2013 to 2015 Myles and Ian worked together to assemble a group of experts from around the world. This book presents the findings of that group and lays out a path to extraordinary performance, fulfilment and enjoyment – a path available to everyone.

Endnotes

1. Gallup, *The State of the American Manager: Analytics and Advice for Leaders* (2015) p. 8.
2. Chartered Management Institute, Unlocking the Potential of the UK Workforce: CMI Policy Paper on Future Skills and Retraining (2020) p. 3.
3. Gallup, *The State of the American Manager: Analytics and Advice for leaders* (2015) p. 2.
4. Chartered Management Institute, https://www.managers.org.uk/knowledge-and-insights/article/nearly-half-of-managers-failed-to-receive-any-training-in-2015/.
5. Thomas H Davenport, *The Fad that Forgot People* (Fast Company, 31st October 1995) https://www.fastcompany.com/26310/fad-forgot-people.
6. Frederick Winslow Taylor, *The Principles of Scientific Management* (New York: Harper & Brothers, 1911), pp. 13–14.
7. https://explore-education-statistics.service.gov.uk/find-statistics/participation-measures-in-higher-education/2018-19.
8. Taylor Nicole Rogers, "Meet Eric Yuan, the Founder and CEO of Zoom, Who Has Made Over $12 Billion since March and Now Ranks among the 400 Richest People in America" (Business Insider), last modified 9 September 2020, https://www.businessinsider.com/meet-zoom-billionaire-eric-yuan-career-net-worth-life.
9. Jennifer Alsever, "Your Company Could Be Spying on You: Surveillance Software Use Up over 50% since Pandemic Started" (Fortune), last modified 1 September 2021, https://fortune.com/2021/09/01/companies-spying-on-employees-home-surveillance-remote-work-computer.

10. See, for example, Bobby Duffy, Hannah Shrimpton and Michael Clemence, *Millennial Myths and Realities* (Ipsos MORI, 2017), accessed 23 February 2022, https://www.ipsos.com/sites/default/files/2017-05/ipsos-mori-millennial-myths-realities-full-report.pdf.

11. "How to Keep Millennials from Leaving" (Accendre), last modified 25 January 2022, https://acendre.com/blog/posts/what-millennials-want-at-work-why-they-might-leave-jobs.

12. Corey Seemiller and Meghan Grace, *Generation Z: A Century in the Making* (Abingdon: Routledge, 2019).

13. Aaron Hurst, *The Purpose Economy* (La Vergne: Elevate, 2014).

14. Flora Holmes, *Public Attitudes to Military Interventionism* (The British Foreign Policy Group, 2020), accessed 23 February 2022, https://bfpg.co.uk/2020/01/public-attitudes-to-uk-military-interventionism.

15. James D. Sharpe Jr and Thomas E. Creviston, "Understanding Mission Command" (US Army), last modified 30 April 2015, https://www.army.mil/article/106872/understanding_mission_command.

16. James D. Sharpe Jr and Thomas E. Creviston, "Understanding Mission Command" (US Army), last modified 30 April 2015, https://www.army.mil/article/106872/understanding_mission_command.

17. L. David Marquet, *Turn the Ship Around! A True Story of Turning Followers into Leaders* (London: Portfolio Penguin, 2015), pp. 3-47.

18. James D. Sharpe Jr and Thomas E. Creviston, "Understanding Mission Command" (US Army), last modified 30 April 2015, https://www.army.mil/article/106872/understanding_mission_command.

19. James D. Sharpe Jr and Thomas E. Creviston, "Understanding Mission Command" (US Army), last modified 30 April 2015, https://www.army.mil/article/106872/understanding_mission_command.

20. L. David Marquet, *Turn the Ship Around! A True Story of Turning Followers into Leaders* (New York: Penguin, 2015).

21. Joel Peterson, *Entrepreneurial Leadership: The Art of Launching New Ventures, Inspiring Others, and Running Stuff* (Nashville: HarperCollins, 2020).

22. Timothy Gallwey, *The Inner Game of Work: Overcoming Mental Obstacles for Maximum Performance* (London: Random House, 2000), p. 17.

23. Mihaly Csikszentmihalyi, *Flow: The Psychology of Optimal Experience* (London: Ebury Publishing, 2002).

24. Myles Downey, *Enabling Genius: A Mindset for Success in the 21st Century* (London: LID Publishing, 2016), pp. 151–168.

25. Timothy Gallwey, *The Inner Game of Work: Overcoming Mental Obstacles for Maximum Performance* (New York: Random House, 2001)

26. Mihaly Csikszentmihalyi, *Flow: The Psychology of Optimal Experience* (London: Random House, 2002).

27. Michael Bungay Stanier, *The Advice Trap: Be Humble, Stay Curious and Change the Way You Lead Forever* (Toronto: Box of Crayons Press, 2020).

28. Widely attributed to Alan Keith, c. 2009.

29. Simon Sinek, *Start with Why* (New York: Portfolio, 2009).

30. Dan Pontefract, *The Purpose Effect: Building Meaning in Yourself, Your Role and Your Organization* (La Vergne: Elevate, 2016).

31. Harrison Owen, *Wave Rider: Leadership for High Performance in a Self-Organizing World* (San Francisco: Berrett-Koehler, 2008).

32. Giulia Pines, "The OKR Origin Story" (What Matters), last modified 6 April 2018, https://www.whatmatters.com/articles/the-origin-story.

33. Glenn Elliott and Debra Corey, *Build It: The Rebel Playbook for World-Class Employee Engagement* (Chichester: Wiley, 2018).

34. John Doerr, *Measure What Matters* (New York: Penguin, 2018).

35. Myles Downey, *Effective Modern Coaching* (London: LID Publishing, 2014), p. 39.

36. Myles Downey, *Effective Modern Coaching* (London: LID Publishing, 2014), p. 43.

37. Myles Downey, *Effective Modern Coaching* (London: LID Publishing, 2014).

38. William Isaacs, *Dialogue: The Art of Thinking Together* (New York: Doubleday, 1999).

39. John Whitmore, *Coaching for Performance*, 5th edn (Boston: Nicholas Brealey, 2017).

40. Timothy Gallwey, *Inner Tennis, Playing the Game*, (London: Random House, 1976) p. 74.

41. Katie Colombus, *How to Listen: Tools for Opening Up Conversations When It Matters Most* (New York: Hachette, 2021).

42. Julie Starr, *The Coaching Manual: The Definitive Guide to the Process, Principles and Skills of Personal Coaching*, 5th edn (Harlow: Pearson, 2021).

43. Tom Kelley and David Kelley, *Creative Confidence: Unleashing the Creative Potential Within Us All* (London: William Collins, 2015).

44. Keith Sawyer, *Group Genius: The Creative Power of Collaboration* (New York: Basic Books, 2007).

45. Jennifer Alsever, "Your Company Could Be Spying on You: Surveillance Software Use Up over 50% since Pandemic Started" (Fortune), last modified 1 September 2021, https://fortune.com/2021/09/01/companies-spying-on-employees-home-surveillance-remote-work-computer.

46. Brené Brown, *Dare to Lead: Brave Work, Tough Conversations, Whole Hearts* (London: Ebury Publishing, 2018).

47. Dan Pontefract, *Lead. Care. Win. How to Become a Leader Who Matters* (Vancouver: Figure 1 Publishing, 2020).

48. George Akerlof and Rachel Kranton, *Identity Economics: How Our Identities Shape Our Work, Wages, and Well-Being* (Princeton: Princeton University Press, 2010).

49. Timothy Gallwey, *The Inner Game of Tennis*, (Pan Books, 2015 Edition), p. 19.

50. Dave Logan, John King and Halee Fischer-Wright, *Tribal Leadership: Leveraging Natural Groups to Build a Thriving Organization* (New York: HarperCollins, 2008).

51. M. Scott Peck, *The Different Drum* (London: Arrow Books, 1990).

52. Bruce Tuckman, "Developmental Sequence in Small Groups," *Psychological Bulletin* 63 (1965): 384–399.

53. Roberto Assagioli, *The Act of Will* (New York: Association for the Advancement of Psychosynthesis, 2007).

54. Carol Dweck, *Mindset: The New Psychology of Success* (New York: Ballantine, 2007).

55. Myles Downey, *Enabling Genius: A Mindset for Success in the 21st Century* (London: LID Publishing, 2016), pp. 30-42.

56. Myles Downey, E*nabling Genius: A Mindset for Success in the 21st Century* (London: LID Publishing, 2016).